Living Vertically

---

*Gospel Sermons
For Lent/Easter
Cycle C*

John N. Brittain

CSS Publishing Company, Inc., Lima, Ohio

LIVING VERTICALLY

Copyright © 2000 by
CSS Publishing Company, Inc.
Lima, Ohio

All rights reserved. No part of this publication may be reproduced in any manner whatsoever without the prior permission of the publisher, except in the case of brief quotations embodied in critical articles and reviews. Inquiries should be addressed to: Permissions, CSS Publishing Company, Inc., P.O. Box 4503, Lima, Ohio 45802-4503.

Scripture quotations are from the *New Revised Standard Version of the Bible*, copyright 1989 by the Division of Christian Education of the National Council of the Churches of Christ in the USA. Used by permission.

Library of Congress Cataloging-in-Publication Data

Brittain, John Neal.
    Living vertically : Gospel sermons for Lent/Easter, Cycle C / John N. Brittain.
      p. cm.
    ISBN 0-7880-1731-4 (alk. paper)
    1. Lenten sermons. 2. Easter—Sermons. 3. Eastertide—Sermons. 4. Bible. N.T. Gospels—Sermons. 5. Sermons. American. I. Title.
BV4277 .B75 2000
252'.62—dc21   00-035799
                                                                                                            CIP

This book is available in the following formats, listed by ISBN:
    0-7880-1731-4   Book
    0-7880-1732-2   Disk
    0-7880-1733-0   Sermon Prep

For more information about CSS Publishing Company resources, visit our website at www.csspub.com.

PRINTED IN U.S.A.

*To the Student Congregations at Neu Chapel
who have challenged me to live vertically*

Table Of Contents

Ash Wednesday   7
Living Horizontally
Matthew 6:1-6, 16-21

Lent 1   13
A Matter Of Means
Luke 4:1-13

Lent 2   19
Three Good Questions
Luke 13:31-35

Lent 3   27
And Now The News
Luke 13:1-9

Lent 4   33
Where Am I?
Luke 15:1-3, 11b-32

Lent 5   39
The Better Part
John 12:1-8

Passion/Palm Sunday   45
A Tale Of Two Crosses
Luke 22:14— 23:56 or Luke 23:1-49

Maundy Thursday   49
Setting The Example
John 13:1-15

Good Friday   55
The Cross: A Symbol Of Absolutes
John 18:1—19:42

Easter Day   59
    Belief Becoming
    John 20:1-18

Easter 2   65
    Believing Is Seeing
    John 20:19-31

Easter 3   71
    Back Where It All Began
    John 21:1-19

Easter 4   75
    The Father And I Are One
    John 10:22-30

Easter 5   81
    Rebecca's Creed
    John 13:31-35

Easter 6   87
    How Can They Do That?
    John 14:23-29

Ascension Of Our Lord   93
    Living Vertically
    Luke 24:44-53

Easter 7   101
    Christo-centric Or Ego-centric?
    John 17:20-26

Ash Wednesday

Living Horizontally

Matthew 6:1-6, 16-21

Mitchell (obviously not his real name) was a pillar of the church I served a quarter century ago and an inspiration to many. A firmly established independent business man, he was in one of those lines of work that depended on a good name, and a high reputation, and he had both. Every year Mitchell would be among the first to turn in his pledge card making whatever adjustment in commitment the finance committee had suggested; he was similarly enthusiastic about special projects.

Back in those days when it was still unusual to do so, a church committee determined that we should add a handicap accessibility ramp to the building. Because it was the desire to have the ramp match the massive stonework of that church, it would be a costly endeavor. True to form Mitchell made the first generous pledge accompanied by a rousing endorsement; we ended up underwriting the cost of the ramp in only a couple of weeks, far ahead of anyone's expectations. Mitchell's early enthusiasm was no doubt a big factor.

There was only one fly in the ointment: Mitchell never gave any money. None; zero; nada; not the first penny. None to the annual budget; zero to special projects; nada toward the handicapped ramp. Because of the polity of that congregation, only a small handful of people were aware of the fact. And yet the truth was that in spite of the notable lack of financial support, his moral support and enthusiasm paid off. From a strictly utilitarian standpoint he probably accomplished more good than some of the widows in the congregation who pledged and gave their mite.

Now this incident from the dim recesses of my past has not exactly preyed on my mind. In fact, I hadn't thought about Mitchell for years until the other day when I was mulling today's text over in my mind. Why not? I have thought about this text frequently since it is one of the traditional readings for Ash Wednesday, is part of Matthew's introduction to the Lord's Prayer, and is just one of those often-cited passages dealing, as it does, with hypocrisy. I guess I had not made the connection because Mitchell didn't really seem to me to be the classic sinister, self-serving hypocrite; the evil, manipulative person so deserving of that epithet. I had not made the connection partly because I had not really done my homework.

While the word "hypocrite," does come to be equated with the worst of the self-serving religious leaders of Jesus' time, even later in Matthew's Gospel, that is not the basic meaning of the term. A hypocrite was, scholars tell us, an actor or interpreter who assumes a role and performs it for the audience's approval. Let me hasten to assure all the theatre majors that I don't find anything repugnant in acting — as long as everyone knows what is going on.

Some years ago we had a theatre major, Kim, who was a very devout conservative Baptist. As a high school senior she had won a big prize from her state Baptist association for a one-woman drama she had written and performed. On Parent's Weekend of her freshman year she had a minor part in a play. Imagine my delight, knowing that her parents would be in the congregation Sunday morning to hear her sing in the choir, seeing her cast as a *prostitute*, complete with short skirt, garish make-up, and showing considerable cleavage. It was with some trepidation that I approached the man I assumed to be her father at the chapel coffee hour the next morning; he was holding a stereotypically large Bible. "How did you enjoy the play?" I squeaked. "I liked it a lot," her father responded, "We have never had any problem separating the daughter from the role." There it was. I was safe.

But what happens when the person and the role are confused? The problem comes in when one is not so much acting as impersonating, assuming an identity that is not one's own and pretending that it is. And that takes us back to Mitchell — what about him? Was he playing a role hypocritically or was he just being who he was — an enthusiastic person with an inability to follow-through, someone with good intentions and little else? When you look at it that way a lot of us are Mitchell's, taking comfort, maybe too much comfort, in Jesus' comment that "the spirit is willing but the flesh is weak."

If part of my problem with this text came from the word "hypocrite," another comes from the action involved: *piety*: "Beware of practicing your piety before others," or as the NIV puts it, "Be careful not to do your 'acts of righteousness' before men...." The term in the Gospel is not just a good deed, or one that has an overall positive effect. It is an act of *righteousness* which is in conformity with the will of God. The main problem is not doing these things in public, in fact just a little earlier in the Sermon on the Mount, Jesus taught us to "let your light shine before others, so that they may see your good works and give glory to your Father in heaven" (Matthew 5:16). The basic issue is not where things are done or who sees them done, but for whom the actions are performed.

This takes us far beyond simple hypocrisy, as popularly understood. In Tillichian terms, it is a question of whether we are living life horizontally or vertically, living superficially or living a life of depth. Over forty years ago the great German/American theologian Paul Tillich wrote an often-cited article in the very popular *Saturday Evening Post* magazine titled, "The Lost Dimension in Religion."[1] (The very fact that a distinguished academician like Tillich was invited to write in this very popular magazine, for which Norman Rockwell often created idyllic cover paintings, is in itself a commentary on some trends in American society.) The lost dimension about which Tillich fretted was the dimension of depth, living life for that which is other than the immediate, loudest, most pressing concern, that world that is "too much with us," of which Auden wrote. Tillich often spoke and wrote about living life in tune with our "ultimate concern," that which is at the deepest and highest levels of our lives. If Tillich was concerned about the frenetic pace of life in 1958 distracting us from what is *really* important, how much more would he have to say to us today, amidst our beepers, cell phones, and hand-held fax machines.

It seems to me that all of this underscores two notions that are of particular urgency for us Americans as we begin a new millenium. First is our place in this world; and second is the question of what effects who and who effects what. I think it is safe to say that for most Christians in most places at most times, there has been a keen sense that this world is not our "native land," our permanent home. Christians have understood themselves, in the words of a song I sang as an adolescent, as "pilgrims and strangers who are tarrying here but a while." While this sense of alienation from the world has sometimes taken unfortunate forms, it has also produced magnificent art, music, liturgy, poetry, and literature. It is the *sehnsucht*, the longing for another home, another shore, that motivated the great fiction of C. S. Lewis.

But for many twenty-first century Americans, this world is very much our home. At Christmas, for instance, it is not the flickering candle-light or smell of incense that makes us feel most at home; it is the frenzy of the malls that lets us know the holy season has really arrived. Easter is not far behind this process of enculturation. This shows up not just in the culture at large but in our churches where there is a constant push to strip worship spaces of traditional symbols and secularize the worship services. I don't want to sound too Grinch-like, but I am not as convinced as many people that "Breakfast with Santa Claus" or an egg hunt with the Easter Bunny are really things that the church needs to sponsor. Leave those to the malls.

The truth is that within our churches as well as in society in general, we no longer have much sense that it is the vertical dimension of life — that which reaches up to God and deep within my soul — that really matters, but the horizontal, that which we see and touch and feel — *and control*. Nothing energizes many congregations like a good remodeling or expansion project and nothing makes us so excited as the news that *the numbers are up*, whichever set of numbers you choose. Is that the ecclesiastical equivalent of going to the mall?

If it is true, as I have suggested, for most Christians in most places at most times, there has been a keen sense of this world not being our "native land," our permanent home, it has been accompanied by the sense that we discover our true selves beyond ourselves: in our relationship with God, in our history as a community of faith, by plumbing the depths of our soul. Today, for most of us, there is a sense that we find our true self at the horizontal level, in pop culture, and that we have it within our own power to invent and re-invent ourselves. I'm not just talking about hair transplants, liposuction, and breast implants; I am thinking about the way in which many of us try to remold our personalities, our values, *who we are.*

There was a time, not long ago, when going off to military service or college presented young adults with a rare, usually once in a life-time, opportunity for a new beginning, to "remake themselves," to start over again with a group of people who did not know their family, their history, their hometown. Today the increased mobility in our society, not to mention the break-up and break-down of families, means that many of us don't even know where home is. For many, life is a constant cycle of new places, new jobs, new people.

The University of Evansville is among a small number of schools to offer students an "Experiential Transcript" that authenticates their participation in various extra- and co-curricular activities. There are many positive reasons for doing this; but one not so positive reason is that many employers have become increasingly skeptical of resumés on which applicants have so "padded" and "shaped" their experiences that it amounts to one big fabrication, a total re-invention of the self. When we look in Scripture, we find the idea that we have been created by God as a unique individual for a purpose; we see the notion of becoming whole, renewed, redeemed and of living life abundantly. Nowhere is there the idea of re-inventing ourselves. It is the difference between living life both vertically and horizontally, in relationship with God and with persons; and with living life totally horizontally, with all our goals, aspirations, values, and our very identity defined by what we see around us.

So was Mitchell a hypocrite or not? I really don't think he was, in the evil, sinister, pharisaical sense. But of course he was in the original sense; he was playing a role, the role of a cheerleader, a good person, totally defined by the horizontal. And he played the role well; he accomplished positive things; almost everyone thought well of him. While his actions may have appeared to be "pious," I don't think he was performing "acts of righteousness" because I don't suppose he had the vertical dimension in life necessary really to perform acts in compliance with God's will. Living his life at the surface, horizontally, even in the church, he stands as a reminder to me of the great danger facing all of us: losing the vertical dimension of faith, the dimension that makes faith real and that makes life real.

Lent 1

A Matter Of Means

Luke 4:1-13

Whenever the Olympics roll around even people like me think a little bit more about fitness and sports. The other day a comedian was talking about healthy living. He had heard a marathon runner describing the joys he derived from the grueling training his sport demanded. There were times, the runner said, when he really got into a zone and felt liberated from the bounds of his body. He felt like he was flying! It is a natural high. "Heck!" (or words to that effect) the comedian responded, "that's why I drink and smoke. I can get lightheaded just huffing and puffing up a flight of stairs."

Well, we smile at that because of two things: we recognize that he has totally misunderstood the "natural high," and more importantly he has missed the significance of the means. Suppose for a minute that smoking and drinking really could produce a temporary "natural high," in addition to the lung cancer, breakup of families, and other goodies they bring in their wake. They would *still* pale in comparison to all the good that a discipline like running accomplishes for the spirit as well as the body.

This silly little example highlights perfectly the underlying dynamic in the story of Jesus' temptation as recorded by Luke. In each case Jesus is tempted with a slight perversion of a legitimate end; but more importantly, in each temptation Satan would have our Lord use means that would betray his mission and purpose in life. This is why this lesson is so commonly read at the beginning of Lent — on Ash Wednesday or today: because it focuses both on the goals of the Christian life, which we sometimes allow to become distorted by the world-view and pressures of the society in which we live; *and* because it encourages us to examine the means we use in striving toward life's goals, no matter how noble they might be.

The first temptation is in some ways the simplest, but also perhaps the most subtle. After forty days of fasting, Jesus is tempted to use his powers to turn a stone into bread. What harm could there be in that? This is, is it not, the same Lord who multiplied a few loaves and fish to feed over 5,000 men, not to mention women and children, and who turned the water into wine. What possible problem could there be in transforming a rock into a little lunch — after forty days!

Obviously there would be no problem in having a little lunch — Jesus did it all the time. Indeed, in the Gospel of John the resurrected Jesus grilled some fish for the disciples' breakfast at the lakeside — no problem. In his response to the Devil, quoting Deuteronomy as he does in every case, Jesus does not say, "One does not need bread at all," or "Only the spiritual is important," he says, "One does not live by bread *alone*."

So whatever else it is, this passage is *not* an endorsement of the ancient heresy of Docetism, the teaching that asserted that Jesus may have appeared to be a human being but, as the fully divine Son of God, could not possibly have inhabited a real human body. He may have *appeared* (*dokeo* in Greek) to suffer and die on the cross, he may have *appeared* to be hungry and thirsty, but he did not really experience those "bodily" pangs. The problem with many of the Docetists was that they not only scoffed at the importance of the Incarnation of Jesus, but also tended to disregard the doctrine of Christian love. Why should we bother to love people's bodies or tend to their physical needs when it is only their spirit that is important?

I recently saw what I would describe as a Docetic commercial on a religious television program. (A program, by the way, which I frequently watch, often with benefit.) The spot began with pictures of emaciated masses of people in some part of the third world. Inspirational music was playing in the background. The words of Matthew 25 scrolled across the screen; "I was hungry and you fed me," and there were images of a huge crusade in a stadium; the evangelist was preaching. Next more words from Matthew 25: "I was thirsty and you gave me drink"; more images from the stadium, with various workers laying their hands on the heads of persons who may have been coming forward in response to an altar call. More words: "Satisfy the hunger and thirst of people — send your donations to," and then the name of the sponsoring parachurch organization. I believe with every fiber of my being that persons need to be fed with the word of God and have their thirst met with the living waters of Jesus Christ welling up in our souls. *But* I also know that in Matthew 25 Jesus is speaking about literal hunger and palpable thirst too. I call this a Docetic commercial because it seemed to imply that what these starving persons need is *only* the gospel message; I would say they need the gospel word *and* the gospel deed of a loaf of bread and cup of water. So if Jesus was concerned about the physical as well as the spiritual (I don't think that Jesus, like most Jews of his time, even conceived of this duality as we do), then what was the problem with turning a rock into bread?

The obvious problem was that of focus. Jesus had not spent forty days and nights fasting and praying in the wilderness in order to be distracted from his great mission at the last moment by focusing on what he was going to eat. And if this was a temptation for Jesus in the wilderness two millennia ago, how much more is it a problem for us with our dayplanners and electronic organizers, people so strapped for time and energy that even W. H. Auden's words about the world being too much with us sound quaintly out of date. Of course Jesus needed something to eat. But this was not the time for it, and certainly not at the expense of beginning his earthly ministry absolutely in tune with his Father.

I imagine we would all agree that living in a nice, attractive community is important. And I have to admit reluctantly that since the advent of big-time gambling in Evansville (with the arrival of a riverboat casino) downtown has perked up quite a bit: a couple of new hotels, some nicer restaurants, and so on. But this raises the issue of "what is a nice, attractive community?" Because I also know that the number of pawn shops and places where you can get cash advances on paychecks you haven't yet earned have multiplied at a much higher rate than nice restaurants. I know that we now have a chapter of Gamblers Anonymous and that all the mental health treatment centers in town find that compulsive gambling and its attendant problems form a substantial part of their caseloads.

I am reminded that when (in the summer of 1996) the local casino made a one-time donation to the local United Way, two agencies turned their share down on moral principles. The Warrick County chapter of the Mental Health Association unanimously voted to refuse the funds. The chapter president explained, "I don't see any sense in using the money that came from gambling to fight gambling," while a member of the board of directors of the United Methodist Youth Home said, "We're dealing with girls whose lives have been broken. My own reaction is that using gambling money to help repair their lives might lead to a misconception. They don't need any more brokenness." Apparently these agencies felt that a community that exploits some for the aggrandizement of others is not as "nice" a community as it may appear.

There is a lot right with having an attractive community, just as there is a lot right with having a good lunch. But both are problematic if the end is misunderstood and if the means undercut the higher purposes of life.

We, as Christians, affirm that Jesus Christ is King of kings and Lord of lords, so what is the problem with the second temptation, that Jesus be given glory and authority over the kingdoms of the world? Clearly, it was the wrong kind of authority and the wrong kind of glory for the one who said to Pilate, "My kingdom is not from this world. If my kingdom were from this world, my followers would be fighting to keep me from being handed over to the Jews. But as it is, my kingdom is not from here" (John 18:36). We are so used to dealing with this world in the ways of the world, this is such a hard contrast to make. If I want to live in a good world, why not legislate morality? If I believe that my way of praying is truly the best, why not work to see to it that everyone in the public school will be coerced to pray my way?

Why not? Because this is not what Jesus' kingdom is all about. It is easy to make this distinction when it appears in its extreme forms, particularly when it appears in other people. We read with regret of the resort to force of arms by great spiritual leaders like Augustine of Hippo and Calvin in Geneva. We should be uncomfortable when we hear words like these:

> *"Remember that the German people are the chosen of God," said Kaiser Wilhelm II. "On me, on me as German Emperor, the Spirit of God has descended. I am His weapon, His sword and His vizard! Woe to the disobedient! Death to cowards!"*

Or these:

> *"I am not here to talk surrender terms, but to talk about how to fight and win the cultural war for the soul of our country ... Our culture is superior because our religion is Christianity ..."* (Pat Buchanan to the Christian Coalition's 1993 "Road to Victory" conference. [quotes from *The Bible Tells Me So*, Anchor Books/ Doubleday, 1996]

No more than Jesus himself, can we obtain control over the world by embracing means of the world that are in conflict with the ways of Christ. Jesus called persons to repentance; he healed the ill, he led the sinner, he excoriated the self-righteous; he did not coerce or use force of arms, and neither should we.

A decade ago my wife and I took a mission group to northeast Brazil to help expand a Methodist Mission in a slum outside the city of Fortaleza. Not long before our departure a number of parents became concerned because of the highly publicized and particularly brutal deaths of a group of American missionaries in the interior of Brazil. A little research was illuminating. The Americans had determined they were going to evangelize a tribe of headhunters (yes, there really are still such groups) in a remote region of the Amazon. They had become aware of the group because of violent skirmishes between the natives and logging interests that were encroaching on their traditional hunting grounds. Local government and Christian groups warned them *not* to approach the already agitated tribe; the sponsoring ministry in the U.S. told them *not* to go; the U.S. State Department ordered them *not* to go. They went anyway and were horribly and brutally killed. Without wanting to seem in the least unkind, one wonders if their action was not tantamount to throwing oneself off the pinnacle of the temple saying, "On their hands they will bear me up." We don't need to look to the jungles of Brazil for examples of this.

A pastor friend's wife has suffered from bouts of depression all her life. A few years ago her physician recommended that she begin taking a minimal dose of an antidepressant. My friend mentioned this at a meeting with other clergy and was roundly denounced; his wife should pray, not be drugged up. This made an already difficult decision even tougher. Happily, she did take the medication and has continued to use it from time to time with very positive results. This is perhaps the most common way I encounter the third temptation of Christ: the temptation to put ourselves in harm's way as a sign of trust in God, either by action or inaction: by what we do (going into the jungle in spite of all kinds of warnings) or by what we fail to do (not taking prescribed medication).

And this takes us back full circle to a variation of Docetism: saying that only the spiritual is important, the physical is of no value: if you believe, you don't need to exercise normal caution, you don't need medical care. The story of Christ's temptations reminds us that we are not disembodied spirits who don't need to worry about our bodies any more than we are merely reductionistically physical machines who can be unconcerned about our spirits. We are complex beings, "fearfully and wonderfully made" by God. Our life of faith is never either/or, it is always both/and. We cannot concentrate so much on the "things" of life that we ignore human and spiritual needs; we cannot become so concerned with external ends that we substitute coercion for compassion. And we must not attempt to manipulate and control God by becoming more spiritual than our Creator intends.

Lent is a time for restoring our balance: internal and external; body and spirit; means and ends. And as believers, we certainly don't want to be like that comedian — mistaking being out of shape for having a "natural high."

Lent 2

Three Good Questions

Luke 13:31-35

My old dog Lou definitely does not belong in the city. Years ago, when my son Tim was in the ninth grade, this skinny dog, who had obviously been scrounging in garbage cans to stay alive, followed him home from school. (Tim has actually acknowledged that he had to carry him part of the way.) We named him Ακαλυφῶν (the one who follows after), Lou for short. He is a mixed breed, but looks and acts like a coon hound. He should be out on a farm somewhere, not chained in a city yard, but that is where he has ended up. (On behalf of parents everywhere, I would like to point out that this is the dog that my son promised he would always feed and care for. Twelve years later my son has two sons of his own, but the old man still has that dog.)

He has never been much of a problem, but a few years ago we had some new folks in the neighborhood who had two large dogs that were barkers. They and Lou would carry on a conversation for hours at a time. A little old lady lived behind us, and the barking would get to her. She, of course, would look out her back window, see Lou howling and call me at home or at the office or leave a message on the answering machine. Dutifully Lou would be brought in, although it usually diminished but did not stop the barking. One day she called when I was working at home, with Lou snoozing at my feet. "Your dog is causing a ruckus, you need to do something, I am going to call the police, etc." Well, this time I had a good answer! I responded, maybe feeling a little too good about it, that Lou was not barking, was snuggled up nice and cozy and that she should call the other neighbors (for a change). This was throwing gasoline on the flame. She retorted that I should be ashamed of myself to lie to her, she could hear my dog, and so on. The truth is, I couldn't blame her skepticism. Lou generally was guilty; she just caught me on an unusually good day.

It is little wonder then, that many people have wondered if the Pharisees were similarly having an uncommonly nice day in today's lesson. After all, they warned Jesus to get out of town because Herod wanted to kill him. They were no doubt correct; Herod certainly did not want religious fanatics causing problems. But the Pharisees as a group have not been friendly before this. In Luke 6:7, when Jesus entered the synagogue where there was a man with a withered hand, we read, "The scribes and the Pharisees watched him to see whether he would cure on the Sabbath, so that they might find an accusation against him." In Luke 11, Jesus was quite critical of the Pharisees because of their scrupulosity over ritual cleanliness. Not surprisingly we are told, "When he went outside, the scribes and the Pharisees began to be very hostile toward him and to cross-examine him about many things, lying in wait for him, to catch him in something he might say" (11:53-54).

Many readers have assumed, like my neighbor, once a barker always a barker, and that the Pharisees could not possibly have had Jesus' interest in mind. The notes in the *Life Application Bible* (Tyndale House, 1986) succinctly summarize this view: "The Pharisees weren't interested in protecting Jesus from danger. They were trying to trap him themselves...." On the other hand, there was no love lost between Herod Antipas (this is the Herod we are talking about here, the one who had executed John the Baptist, not Herod the Great) and the Pharisees. Perhaps they were warning Jesus more out of spite toward Herod than good will toward him, the equivalent of voting against someone rather than for the opponent. And of course it is not beyond comprehension that there were some Pharisees who were receptive to Jesus' message, or at least sympathized with him as a fellow believer in the midst of pagan Roman occupation, and really did want to help him. So this is a good question. Exactly why did the Pharisees warn Jesus about Herod? It may be a good question, but I don't have a good answer.

This is how it always is when we get into analyzing the motivation of others; we never really know. There is the old cartoon of the psychiatrist in an elevator. Someone else gets in and says, "Good Morning." The bubble over the psychiatrist's head shows his thought: "I wonder what he meant by that?" We can and do often over-analyze suggestions, remarks, and advice from others. If we are not careful we get caught by what Martin Luther King, Jr., used to refer to as "the paralysis of analysis." On the one hand this is both understandable and to a degree appropriate. Is someone's advice sincere, really meant to help us? Or is it cunning, meant to make us look stupid and advance their cause? A clergy friend often says that regardless of protestations to the contrary, every United Methodist pastor is in competition with every other United Methodist pastor. (I say this as a United Methodist. I don't suppose we are any better or worse at this than others.) I am sure there is a great deal of truth in this observation. Does that mean, however, that we never help one another, never give sincere advice, never have the best interest of the fellow pastor or his/her congregation at heart? Of course not.

It gets even more complex than that. In academic and corporate settings, I have seen individuals take terrible career advice, accept or decline promotions or relocations, on the recommendation of those who claimed to have their best interest at heart but were clearly, consciously or unconsciously, really thinking of the bottom line of the company or unit. And anyone who has ever attended a Little League or Youth Soccer match has seen parents carrying on in a way that can hardly be described as in the best interest of their children, although they would insist otherwise.

The question of motivation is always a good one and always imponderable. After a worship service one Sunday morning years ago, I overhead a parishioner tell the lay leader, "I didn't agree with what the preacher had to say today." "Neither did I," responded the lay leader. "But you know, I don't always agree with what I say." Why any of us say what we say, do what we do, and act how we act often defies any explanation, even our own.

The third good question (yes, I am skipping the second) in today's story is not so imponderable: Why did Jerusalem have its history of killing the prophet? There is no doubt that it did have a history of killing some prophets like Naboth and Zechariah, and threatening others like Jeremiah. Of course these words would have had a double meaning by the time Luke wrote them down since by then Jesus would have been crucified and Stephen stoned in Jerusalem. Underlying all these deaths — at least partially — is the motive of power and control.

You remember the case of Naboth whose vineyard King Ahab coveted. Queen Jezebel devised a way to get rid of him, calling a solemn fast and having Naboth seated at the head of the table as a kind of authority figure. He was then falsely accused of cursing God, an offense that if true would have merited the death penalty under Moses' prohibition of false prophets. It wasn't true, but it provided the pretense to kill him, giving the king what he wanted in an illegitimate use of royal power (1 Kings 21:8ff). In the latter years of King Joash, who like leaders before and since began his reign well but ended badly, God raised up Zechariah as a prophet to call the people back to faith in God. With less concern for pretense, he was simply stoned at the command of the king he dared challenge, again in a display of royal power (2 Chronicles 24:20ff).

Jeremiah fell somewhere between these two cases and was spared death. He had prophesied against the false confidence the people were placing in the invincibility of Jerusalem, harshly telling them that the Temple would be destroyed. Not surprisingly the priests and court prophets whose life, livelihood, and power base were all tied to the institution of the Temple took drastic exception to this and invoked the death penalty against being a false prophet. Fortunately for Jeremiah, there were cooler heads who remembered that there was a precedent for such nay-saying:

> *Then the officials and all the people said to the priests and the prophets, "This man does not deserve the sentence of death, for he has spoken to us in the name of the LORD our God." And some of the elders of the land arose and said to all the assembled people, "Micah of Moresheth, who prophesied during the days of King Hezekiah of Judah, said to all the people of Judah: 'Thus says the LORD of hosts, Zion shall be plowed as a field;*

> *Jerusalem shall become a heap of ruins, and the mountain of the house a wooded height.' Did King Hezekiah of Judah and all Judah actually put him to death? Did he not fear the LORD and entreat the favor of the LORD, and did not the LORD change his mind about the disaster that he had pronounced against them? But we are about to bring great disaster on ourselves!"*
>
> — Jeremiah 26:16-19

Because we all like happy endings, we often forget than an exact contemporary of Jeremiah's, a prophet by the name of Uriah, proclaimed exactly the same message as Jeremiah and was executed by the king.

Jerusalem, in short, killed prophets because Jerusalem was the center of power and authority, and those in positions of authority don't like to be challenged. In Jesus' day the power structure within Judaism was fractured, leading to increased hostility between the factions and heightened concern by the Romans who didn't want to be troubled dealing with religious uprisings among the Jews. The Pharisees saw themselves as the true custodians of the laws and traditions of Moses, separated from the dominant Roman culture; but it was the Sadducees who controlled the High Priestly office and, while claiming to be super-conservative theologically, willingly played ball with the Roman government. Then there were the Herodians who were quite comfortable making accommodation with the local Roman representatives, and the Zealots who wanted the Romans thrown out. Each group had its own agenda and power base and worked to undermine the others. (Sounds sort of like Washington, D.C., or any state capital, doesn't it?) When we read in Mark 3:6 that the Pharisees conspired against Jesus in league with the Herodians, it was a case of strange bedfellows. These two groups may have agreed on little besides the fact that Jesus was a threat to their individual power base.

If the first good question, that of why the Pharisees warned Jesus, is inscrutable, the third good question is not. Jerusalem had always killed true prophets, because true prophets tended to threaten, question or condemn the *status quo*, something those in power can never tolerate. Then what about the middle and central question in this set of three: Why did Jesus reject the warning to flee from Herod Antipas?

Here, there is no question. Jesus' answer is clear: he had an agenda, a life mission that could not be thwarted by the real threats posed by Herod, that sly and crafty "fox," or Jerusalem, a focus of power historically opposed to those like Jesus. In the synoptic Gospels we see Jesus' public life very roughly divided into three phases: a public ministry dominated by healings and great crowds; a more private ministry focusing on instructing the twelve and the seventy; and the week of the Passion toward which we inexorably move during Lent. Perhaps Jesus' reference to "today, tomorrow, and the next day," alludes to this division. In any case it is clear that Jesus had ample opportunity to alter his course, change his tactics and methods, if self-preservation was his priority.

It is customary on Maundy Thursday, as Lent draws to its climax, to meditate on Jesus' prayer on the Mount of Olives, "Father, if you are willing, remove this cup from me; yet, not my will but yours be done," (Luke 22:42) and realize that Jesus could have walked away. Today's lesson, on the second Sunday in Lent, reminds us that there were many occasions in his ministry — would it be too much to say daily occasions? — when Jesus could have walked away. He was not naïve; he knew of the religious turmoil that surrounded him; he knew of Jerusalem's sordid history with prophetic voices. But he had a mission. Jesus calls us to take up our cross daily to follow him. We may forget that it was a daily decision for him as well. "I must be on my way," says Jesus.

In Luke's Gospel, we find a summary of Jesus' self-understanding of his mission in his own words. (See *The New Interpreter's Bible*, Vol. 9, p. 281, Abingdon, 1995.)

> *He said to them, "Why were you searching for me? Did you not know that I must be in my Father's house?"*
> — Luke 2:49

> *But he said to them, "I must proclaim the good news of the kingdom of God to the other cities also; for I was sent for this purpose."*
> — Luke 4:43

"The Son of Man must undergo great suffering, and be rejected by the elders, chief priests, and scribes, and be killed, and on the third day be raised."
— Luke 9:22

"Yet today, tomorrow, and the next day I must be on my way, because it is impossible for a prophet to be killed outside of Jerusalem." — Luke 13:33

When Jesus came to the place, he looked up and said to him, "Zacchaeus, hurry and come down; for I must stay at your house today ... For the Son of Man came to seek out and to save the lost." — Luke 19:5, 10

"For I tell you, this scripture must be fulfilled in me, 'And he was counted among the lawless'; and indeed what is written about me is being fulfilled."
— Luke 22:37

So, as the prayer in the garden reminds us, Jesus was neither unaware of nor oblivious to the dangers he faced from ill wishers within the religious community and government officials more concerned with order than justice. But he was steadfast in his faithfulness to God. If we, indeed, are to deny ourselves, take up our crosses every day, and follow Jesus (see Luke 9:23), we must have a similar dedication. Kierkegaard captured this spirit in the profound title of his book *Purity of Heart Is To Will One Thing.* We will face no less opportunities to diverge off the path than did Jesus; our reasons may be far less compelling than his. Few of us face persecution and death for our faith: maybe a little unpopularity; perhaps a difficult decision; inevitably some discomfort.

We all face these three good questions constantly. First, why are people giving me this advice? What is their motivation? Is it really for my own good, or is it to serve their needs? Do I really need to buy this product, use this service; even if it is good advice, should I take it, or are there other priorities, other goals that are more important? Third, are there forces, systems, philosophies, structures that are mitigating against my actions? Of course there are and always have been. No matter how much we may try to idealize the old days, there has never been a time in human history when goodness, justice, equality, and faithfulness have not been challenged. There have always been power structures and systems that oppose the prophetic voice, that is any voice that articulates the word and will of God. These "powers and principalities" (Ephesians 6:12 KJV) continue to silence the prophets using whatever means are available.

It is the middle question that is most decisive — the question of whether or not we opt out of the Christian life or remain faithful to our calling. This is the crucial one. This does not mean that every decision will be obvious or easy. But it does mean we know the direction in which we need to proceed: the direction of faithful service, loving sacrifice, and steadfast obedience.

You may recall the controversy of a few years ago about the appropriateness of football players kneeling in prayer after a touchdown. Former President Jimmy Carter (is supposed to have) made this observation:

> *It's kind of easy to bow down in the end zone, but the real test of my character is, can I bow down to God on a Monday when millions of people are not watching and the stands aren't packed and my wife is not necessarily saying I am a superstar and my little boy is late for school? Can I stand for Christ when adversity comes my way? Can I stand for him on that day?*

We do live in a confusing world, a world of competing demands and mixed messages. But as we follow Jesus Christ on our Lenten journey, we can always respond, "Today, tomorrow, and the next day I must be on my way."

Lent 3

And Now The News

Luke 13:1-9

I know that they didn't have CNN or Walkmen back in Jesus' day, but if they had, they would have been listening to the World Report in today's Gospel Lesson. The topic is current events and things surely haven't changed much in 2,000 years because the headline stories are bad news: the imperial troops senselessly murder a few peasants; a tower collapses and kills eighteen. "What do you think about that?" Jesus asks. "Do you think that those poor folks who ended up dead were worse sinners than everybody else?" There is an uneasy silence. "No," he answers his own rhetorical question. "No, I tell you, but unless you repent, you will all perish as they did."

How about those Iraqis who were incinerated in the air-raid shelter in Baghdad on Ash Wednesday a few years ago — were they worse sinners than all the other Iraqis? And the Azerbaidzhanis or Croats or Kenyans who are caught in the crossfire of civil war — are they worse sinners than those who live in countries that are at peace this week? And the victims of AIDS, dying lonely, painful deaths — because they are suffering in this way, does that mean that they are worse sinners than all the rest of us? There are certainly people who feel that way — or at least act that way. "No, I tell you," says Jesus, " but unless you repent, you will all perish as they did."

What an astounding response! Wouldn't you expect Jesus to condemn the brutality of the oppressors? After all, those Galileans that Pilate slaughtered were Jesus' countrymen, and such cruelty was not unusual for Pilate: he had slaughtered some Samaritans as they worshiped at their temple on Mount Gerezim; another time, he had several Jews killed because of their opposition to his taking offerings left at the Jerusalem temple. Surely such tyranny demands an outcry of protest, perhaps a call for revolutionary counterviolence — or, at the very least, appeals for U.N. economic sanctions.

My brother, the attorney, would sarcastically say that the story about the tower collapsing is the kind of thing lawyers like to hear: no doubt the builders should be brought to court for unsafe construction practices; or maybe there was a building inspector on the take. But Jesus tells us that such tragic events, some caused willfully, others unfortunate accidents, should be occasions not for judgment or for speculation, but for *repentance:* "Unless you repent," Jesus says, " you will all perish as they did." What does that mean?

One of the constant problems in trying to capture the bombshell quality of much of Jesus' teaching is that the biblical images and language have become domesticated, or taken on such stuffy "religious" overtones that they lose their power. The central point of all Jesus' teaching is that each of us must experience *metanoia,* generally translated by the religious-sounding English words "repentance" or "conversion." This common Greek word *metanoia* literally meant "to change one's mind" but in everyday use had come to mean "to turn around and change direction." It is the word you would use if you were traveling down the road and remembered you had left something at home — you would turn around and go a different way. Mark begins his story of Jesus by telling us, "Jesus came to Galilee proclaiming the good news of God, and saying, "The time is fulfilled, and the kingdom of God has come near; *repent,* and believe in the good news" (Mark 1:14b-15). If we are to discover the good news that Jesus has for us, in other words, if we are to become participants in God's reign and God's good will for the world, we need to begin to see things from a totally different perspective, we need to come at everyday events in a new and different and exciting way.

And one of the first things we need to change is our tendency to imagine that we can judge from appearances: to think that if someone suffers, "They had it coming to them," and that if they prosper, "God is blessing them." Because this is such a natural inclination, the Scriptures are full of warnings against. it. My personal favorite is the classic statement in Ecclesiastes: "... the race is not to the swift, nor the battle to the strong, nor bread to the wise, nor riches to the intelligent, nor favor to the skillful; but time and chance happen to them all" (9:11).

Jesus made the same point in the Sermon on the Mount: "But I say to you, Love your enemies and pray for those who persecute you, so that you may be children of your Father in heaven; for he makes his sun rise on the evil and on the good, and sends rain on the righteous and on the unrighteous" (Matthew 5:44-45).

In spite of such warnings, we make superficial judgments all the time, just as much as those to whom Jesus was speaking in Luke 13. How else could we fight wars or sponsor terrorism, if we didn't believe deep down this year's enemies "have it coming to them"? One of the justifications for colonialism, foreign domination, and economic exploitation is that we look at countries or regions which are "underdeveloped" and assume that the underdevelopment is because of shortcomings — the "sinfulness" if you will — of the local people: they must be "undevelopable." And so, given this state of affairs, we have every right to go in and show these local yokels how to do things correctly and, while we are at it, to take the best resources for ourselves.

If you go into a florist shop virtually anywhere in the U.S. this week and buy a bunch of fresh cut flowers, especially roses, the odds are very good that they will have been grown in Zimbabwe, a half globe away. This beautiful and mountainous country is now the world's second largest producer of fresh cut flowers after Holland. What a glorious sight to stand, as I have, and look at Zimbabwean valleys stretching as far as the eye can see filled with flowers, cultivated for the world market. How fascinating it is to think of how these vast carpets of color will soon be loaded aboard refrigerated jumbo jets and on their way to Cologne, Paris, London, Chicago. The less beautiful thought is that much of the traditional farm land on which these flower farms have been developed is now owned by multinational corporations which employ the local persons not as farmers, but as minimally paid workers.

Perhaps you've read in the papers about food shortages in Southern Africa. The articles tell how Zimbabwe, always an exporter of food, is now having to import staples, putting a strain on its economy. President Mugabe has cited the current drought, which is certainly one factor. But another factor has been the conversion of farmland which traditionally provided food and locally controlled cash crops to the cultivation of flowers, a commodity whose price is wholly controlled by foreign interests. So if in the coming months you see pictures of Zimbabweans going hungry, or hear of unrest in that country due to food shortages or a bad economy, does that mean that these people are worse sinners than other people, worse sinners than us? "Of course not," Jesus says, "but unless *you* repent...."

And now Jesus brings us to the painful part of *metanoia*, of seeing things from God's point of view. It is cheap and easy to criticize others, to make presumptions about them based on circumstance. It is desperately painful to look at ourselves. What part do I play in economic systems that exploit other people? How do I perpetuate attitudes that demean others? How have I contributed to the pain or suffering or downfall of another person — a friend, a fellow student, an unnamed homeless person I have never met, a farmer half-way around the world?

So stories about the misfortune of others are not cause for us to gloat or to assume they brought these things on themselves. Neither are they neutral stories that we can shrug off as we switch from CNN to ESPN. They are wake-up calls to each of us to examine our hearts, our relationship with God, and our involvement with other people. Do we lift others up, or just ignore them, or actually pull other people down?

Jesus continued with the familiar parable of the barren fig tree — one that recurs in various forms throughout Scripture. "You will know them by their fruits," Jesus used to say about individuals as well as groups of people. So you don't have to be a literature major to understand what this parable is about. The fig tree has not produced fruit, so it might as well be cut down. But the gardner wants to give it one more chance: a little more cultivation, a little more mulch, a little more time. And if there is no fruit next year....

And so it is for all of us. We are being given care and nurture and time. Jesus Christ, God's gardnener, is offering us every opportunity for *metanoia*, to begin to see the world from God's point of view. When we hear the news, when we read of the misfortunes of others, we must not fall into the trap of thinking that we are somehow fundamentally different from them, but must realize that we are fundamentally the same. "Unless you repent," Jesus says.

During the season of Lent, when we pay special attention to the process of nurturing our spirits and cultivating our Christian life, the parable of the fig tree has a special, positive meaning, with its promise for the future. But this gospel text as a whole is a sobering warning against complacency and self-righteousness. It is a call to serious self-examination and being open to the life-transforming power of God, so that we begin to see other people and the whole world not from our own narrow perspective, but from God's point of view.

Lent 4

Where Am I?

Luke 15:1-3, 11b-32

I suppose we are all a little bit nervous about the prospect of a sermon on a Bible story as familiar and sometimes as overworked as the Parable of the Prodigal Son. "What can I possibly say that hasn't been said before?" And I know what's going through your minds: "Are we going to be subjected to the same old sermon yet another time?" Confronting a familiar Bible passage like this mid-Lent really serves to address the discipline of reading Scripture as part of our devotional life, particularly passages that are very familiar. On the one hand there is always the danger of mentally turning off: "Oh, I've heard that before." On the other hand, there is the occupational hazard of preachers of recognizing a passage as a familiar one and so looking for some bizarre twist or particle of Bible trivia that will spark it up and make it interesting. Neither is appropriate. We always come to the Scriptures with a sense of expectation that if we really attend to what is there, there will be some word from God for us. So in the middle of Lent, what is there here for us?

A good place to start is always the context, and if we look at Luke 15 we see that there are three parables about things lost and found. Verses 3-7 is the "story of the lost sheep," which of course is not about sheep at all but about *the shepherd* who seeks the sheep, finds it, and restores it to the fold. Then verses 8-10 is the "story of the lost coin," but again it is not really a story about money, but rather about a *woman* who loses the coin and who turns her house upside down until she finds it. When it is found, she is so joyful that she can't just keep it to herself, so she invites her friends in to celebrate. Jesus says, that the angels in heaven rejoice that way over one lost sinner who repents.

So when we get to 15:11 in its own context, we are naturally expecting another story about the recovery of the lost, and we are not disappointed, for the story begins, "There was a *man* who had two sons," and sure enough one of them is soon lost. Obviously, then, at least some of the focus of this parable will be on the father and how he handles the fact that his son has been lost. But this does not turn out to be a story exclusively about the "los*er*." After all the "los*ee*" is neither an inanimate object nor a dumb animal (I have had bad experiences with sheep). And there are other people involved: a brother and a group of servants.

The father in the parable clearly represents some divine attributes, just as the shepherd and the woman in the earlier parables personify God's search for the lost. What are some of the characteristics we see in this father? On the one hand, we can say that the father was really the cause of the younger son's problems: had he not given the younger son the inheritance ahead of time there would be no story. But on the other hand, the father is both fair-minded and generous. It was unusual to distribute an inheritance before one's death, but it was not unheard of. The father apparently yielded to his son's request for his share of the wealth before it was really due him out of simple kindness. Assuming that these were the father's only two sons, the share given to the younger would have been one third of his total worth, so the father was giving up a significant source of income and security, but not the whole farm.

We know that human motivations are complex, but if there were any factors other than kindness and generosity at work, Jesus doesn't mention them. Manipulation, threats, and cunning are all present in some Gospel parables, but not here. If the father had second thoughts about the wisdom of his action, we are not told. If he worried about his son's freedom, it did not affect his course of action. He simply gave his son resources and independence. I must confess finding it tiresome the way that some people attempt to blame God for their personal problems or the nation's problems or the world's problems. This is the equivalent of saying that the father was to blame for his son's problems because of his generosity.

Of course it is true, but do we really want it any other way? By allowing humankind free-will, individuality, and creativity, God has allowed the possibility of abandoning the good, misusing our time and talent, and being caught in a web of evil. That is the flip side of generosity and freedom. But would any of us really prefer a world of "fail safe" determinism, some kind of lock-step double predestination?

It is this same kind and generous father who sees the failed son from afar and welcomes him home, refusing to allow him to feel humiliation and act out his shame. His exultation over the return to life of this "dead" son and his use of all the symbolic behavior — the fatted calf, the ring, the new garments, and the great banquet — all remind us of how much he loved and cared for this son. Providing freedom and independence can sometimes be construed as a lack of caring, as simply "turning one out," throwing them in the deep end of life and hoping they don't drown. Throughout Scripture we are reminded that it is God's desire that people be set free, not that they be set adrift.

Here is where heavy-handed comparisons between this and the foregoing two parables of lost and found break down. The sheep and the coin were naturally recovered solely through the efforts of the shepherd and the woman, as would be wholly appropriate with an animal and an inanimate object. But the younger son had to undergo a personal transformation before he could be found: in an important sense he had to "find himself." While it is tempting to read sinister or disrespectful motivations into his request for his inheritance, there is really no reason to: he simply wanted to be on his own, to be independent, to make his own way. He was thinking of himself, to be sure, but in a way that we Americans tend to applaud: he had get-up-and-go, entrepreneurial spirit.

After he got-up-and-went things did not pan out; he found himself at the point of ultimate degradation for a Jew: amongst the swine. Verse 17 says that he "came to himself" using one of Luke's medical phrases that suggests a person returning to his right mind after illness or delirium. He recognized that he was lost and determined that he wanted to return home. This reminds us of an important dynamic of salvation, whether in the ultimate sense of salvation from sin or salvation from a destructive behavior or addiction, or salvation from an unwholesome relationship: no one can force salvation upon someone or manipulate another into salvation. Each one must come to terms with one's own need for salvation. There was no seventeenth chorus of "Just As I Am" as the father tried to force the son to come back; but when the son recovered his senses the father was waiting.

Now the older brother becomes obvious, or is it obnoxious? He cannot contain his jealously and resentment over the luxurious treatment given his wayfaring brother. I totally understand his feelings: he had been the good boy, and sometimes the one who stays at home and does what is expected is overlooked and taken for granted. But the father's obvious concern for maintaining their relationship and his assurance that "all that is mine is yours" seems to make that unlikely. The more we look at the older brother the more we realize that he too seems to have wandered from his father not in physical proximity, but in attitude and outlook. Like his younger brother, he too seems to be thinking only of himself, but he covers it more effectively with a thin veneer of piety and respect.

If his jealousy of the joyful reception is somewhat understandable, bitter self-righteousness is less so. His accusation that the brother had "devoured your living with harlots" is surprising since the story doesn't mention this salacious detail. He was self-pitying: "You never gave me a kid." Jealously, meanness, self-righteousness, and self-pity all come from an inwardly directed vision that judges all things from the perspective of how what is happening is going to affect *me*. It is selfishness masked as piety.

The elder brother has many descendants in American society. He may be a leader: a church officer, a highly visible volunteer, a key citizen who lets us know what she or he has sacrificed on behalf of the group. They are always around, doing good things, so we are surprised when their narrow and inwardly-focused vision slips out. Suddenly some breaking point arrives and the bitterness pours out. They seem to need to think ill of others, to point out their flaws and weaknesses, and to dwell on the problems others are causing them. There is no patience with those who make mistakes they feel they have avoided. The elder brother personifies a legalistic attitude, whether that of the Pharisees or of ourselves: an attitude that does things that are perceived as correct — "These many years I have served you" — without the proper motivation. The brother was right in a way, but so what? He overlooked what was really important: "... this your brother was dead, and is alive; he was lost, and is found." Proper conduct without devotion of the heart to God and persons easily degenerates into legalism.

There is an often overlooked but important group in this parable: the servants of the household of the father and sons. They are no Greek chorus, but they are specifically mentioned in three places. First, it is the son's reminiscence of how these servants were treated in his father's house that helped him "come to his senses." They had better than hog-slop to eat and their ordinary day-to-day routine was preferable to his life of adventure gone sour. The second time they appear is to follow the father's directions to prepare the celebration for the returned son. Then it is one of the servants who explains what is happening to the elder brother, much to his dismay.

Our American (Protestant?) approach to things tends to be so intensely individualistic and personal that we immediately hone in on the prodigal — the individual gone wrong. We force ourselves to look at the father and brother but forget about the role the anonymous group plays. How many times we have read testimonials of persons who have "been brought to themselves" by the simple, inconspicuous often unconscious witness of the people of God, by the individual whose life of quiet faith was observed from a distance and recognized as better than the slop that was being accepted.

We are reminded that as Christians our role is always to be like that of these servants of facilitating the return of the prodigal by faithfully going about our tasks without resentment or special recognition: doing God's will, making ready the celebration. This makes it doubly unfortunate when we find ourselves aligned with the sour grapes of the older brother instead of making ready the feast to welcome back the penitent and forgiven.

It is a servant who explains to the older son what the feasting is about, even though he doesn't want to hear. One of the inescapable teachings of Scripture is that we believers are called upon to tell what God is doing, to tell the story of grace and freedom, of redemption, forgiveness, and acceptance, even when those who have wrapped themselves in a cloak of self-righteousness do not want to hear. It is these inconspicuous servants at each point in the story who allow the action to proceed by faithful living, by faithful obedience, and by faithful proclamation.

Maybe there is more to this story than some of us remember. It has a great deal to say about human emotions and dynamics, far beyond the folly and repentance of the younger son. There is the generosity, the love, and the hope of the father; the resentment and selfishness of the older brother; and the quiet but crucial lives of the servants. This gives us much to ponder during Lent as we consider our motivations and emotions. Have we *really* come to terms with who we are and our relationship with God? Where am I in this story? Am I lost, settling for some hog slop rather than the good things my father wants me to enjoy? Am I playing the role of the older brother, doing right things for the wrong reason, full of suspicion and resentment? Or am I playing the role of faithful servant of the Father: inconspicuous perhaps, but having an influence far beyond what I may realize? These are good questions for the middle of Lent.

Lent 5

The Better Part

John 12:1-8

Some of the most impressive people I have ever met are missionaries. This is not because of some misdirected romantic notion I have about mission work but because of who these people are, what they are doing and, perhaps as important, what they could be doing. Let me give a few examples.

Some years ago I took a mission team to work in Conjuncto Palmieras, a favella or slum of about 10,000 inhabitants outside the northeast Brazilian city of Fortaleza. There we met Lawrence and Judy Fetter. Larry was a pastor in the United Church of Canada who had had a successful career and, in mid-life, was serving a large suburban congregation. His wife was a writer of children's literature. Then they determined that they wanted to do something more for the Lord, something different, so they applied for mission service. To make a long story short, by the time we met them they had gone through language school and were serving several small Methodist Churches, freeing Brazilian national pastors to serve larger congregations. They were building their own home in the Conjuncto, which at that point was really a squatters' village writ large, making them not just the first missionaries to do so, but the first pastor who would actually live among the people.

In recent years I have taken more than one group to the "Give Ye Them To Eat" program, a rural development ministry in the remote Mexican village of Tlancualpian, population 3,000. The program was begun and continues to be led by an American lay missionary couple, Terry and Muriel Henderson. Terry is an agronomist by training, Muriel an educator. They are both renaissance people doing whatever needs to be done in a multifaceted ministry that includes faith development, agricultural improvement, health education, and much more.

Nor does one have to look to foreign countries. Here in Evansville the Reverends Calvin and Nelia Kimbrough have labored in the inner city at Patchwork Central, an intentional Christian community they helped found two decades ago. Calvin is a talented photographer and videographer and Nelia is an artist. I am confident that with their gifts and graces they could have served in a variety of settings or pursued successful careers in the media and the arts.

The point is that in each of these cases — and many others that any one of us could provide — these individuals who are serving God by serving the poor — could be doing many other things, things that some people would argue would be more appropriate and more valuable.

Perhaps as a successful pastor of an affluent suburban congregation, the Reverend Fetter could have raised untold sums of money to go toward mission work; perhaps he could have supported several missionary families had he stayed in the parish. The Hendersons could be successful farmers or otherwise engaged in agribusiness in their home state of Arizona, sending machinery and food and money to Mexico, perhaps occasionally taking a week or two to provide hands-on experience in the field.

Now if these suggestions sound unkind or far-fetched, let me suggest that's only because we are sitting here in a worship service, because, in fact, such critiques are made all the time. Virtually any time we have prepared to take a mission team anywhere, in this country or abroad, someone has sincerely asked, "Couldn't you do more good just by sending the money?" The answer to that question depends, of course, on how your define "more good." Obviously you can buy more nails or paint with funds that are not spent on airfare or food; but you do not have the human interaction; you do not communicate the witness of care and Christian love by not being there. And over the years I have had any number of students whose family and friends have been less than overjoyed to learn of their intention to enter the ministry or go into mission work or some other "helping" profession rather than engage in a more lucrative career. You can recite the arguments about "doing good by doing well," sending money, supporting helping agencies, etc, etc. The persons in question have sometimes gone one way, sometimes another.

"Why was this perfume not sold for three hundred denarii and the money given to the poor?" That is not a bad question; and certainly not one that has stopped being asked. A lot of good for a lot of people could have been done with almost a year's pay for an average laborer. God does need good business people who send donations to the church as well as clergy, doesn't God? So this familiar tableau from John 12 is not all that outdated. There is the pious Mary sitting at Jesus' feet as she had done on at least one other occasion, according to Luke 12; and there is the money-grubbing betrayer Judas, salivating over the money that he would like to put into the common purse where he can filch it!

When we put it in those almost caricature-like terms it is easy to translate it with pious me (or pious you) in the role of Mary, sitting at Jesus' feet; and some evil secular humanists (or at least misinformed bleeding-heart liberals) saying, "No, don't do that! Don't serve the Lord!" But when we look a little closer and see a more nuanced story, it may be a little less clear about exactly where we fit in.

Because, of course, John 12 is not the only place there is a story like this. The other Gospels have similar stories; similar enough that some readers feel that today's lesson is simply a doublet, a slight variant of the same story; others think the discrepancies are significant enough that there were two episodes of women washing Jesus' feet. Whichever interpretation is more congenial to you, it was not just Judas who raised the objection about the waste: in Matthew it is the "disciples" who became angry and objected; in Mark it was "some" who were there who were perplexed. It was not just Judas; it was "some," "some of the disciples." And in any case it wasn't just somebody washing Jesus' feet and somebody objecting to it; Martha was there, serving as usual, and the recently resuscitated Lazarus is at the table. A more variegated scene than we might remember it.

This slightly more complex cast of characters makes me think of the interpretation of this story found in the late Medieval classic, *The Cloud of Unknowing*, written, I think, in response to some overly-systematized approaches to spiritual growth, like Walter Hilton's *The Ladder of Perfection*, a kind of fourteenth-century version of the "Four Spiritual Laws." As the title indicates, the author believed that there is much about God that we don't know and can't know in this life, our knowledge of God is obscured by this "cloud of unknowing." This is not a negative thing, like the "Dark Night of the Soul," it is simply a reminder of our human limitations; the Christian life cannot be reduced to a simple set of propositions.

But the anonymous author of *The Cloud* knew that people find themselves in various circumstances and at different levels of spiritual maturity in this life. In broad terms he could talk about the active life, symbolized in the Luke story by Martha, busy doing many things, and the contemplative life of sitting at the feet of Jesus exemplified by Mary, much to Martha's annoyance. But as much as he wanted to avoid the appearance of a simple plan or scheme, he wrote of both the active and contemplative lives having two levels, with the upper level of the active life being more or less the same as the lower level of the contemplative life. What he was getting at is that at the lowest level of the active life (where I suspect many of us live most of the time) we are so caught up in the frenzy of stuff that Jesus is not on our minds and God is not really part of our lives. At the highest level of the contemplative life we are in full communion with God: this is the perfection we Methodists talk about going on toward; we attain it only in the next life.

Most of us, of course, are somewhere in the middle striving on toward perfection but also backsliding. It would be grossly unfair to characterize Martha as an unbeliever. Recall how, in the story of the raising of Lazarus, she had left Mary and those who had come to console her and her sister, and gone out to meet Jesus with the words, "Lord, if you had been here, my brother would not have died. But even now I know that God will give you whatever you ask of him." These were not the words of someone so preoccupied with the cares of daily life that she had no awareness of Jesus' identity. Nor should we cast Mary in the role of stained-glass window saint simply because she was in the right place doing the best thing on two occasions. She, too, no doubt had her shortcomings; none of us are perfect in this life. But how about those others — Judas, disciples, some — who objected to what Mary was doing? Where do they fit in? Let me make a suggestion.

If *The Cloud of Unknowing* was written partially in response to works like *The Ladder of Perfection*, I think it was also written in response to one of the religious superstars of fourteenth century England, Richard Rolle. I love Richard Rolle because he is what my mother calls, "A good example of a bad example," and because he embodied the spirit of many university students (and some clergy) I have known over the years.

Rolle dropped out of Oxford University at the age of nineteen with the intention of becoming a hermit. Fashioning a makeshift robe out of two of his sister's tunics and his father's rain-hood, he became a kind of freelance, self-styled hermit. I have no doubt that he had some real, powerful religious experiences, one of which he described as a warmth in his chest that reminds me of John Wesley's heart-warming Aldersgate experience. It is also clear from his writings (in *The Fire of Love*) that he had an enormous opinion of himself. He had no spiritual director and had absolutely no intention of getting one because he felt he was spiritually far advanced beyond those around him and really needed no advice. He heard sweet heavenly music which made it impossible for him to enjoy the singing in church which paled in comparison. He had visions, joys, and glories in the Holy Spirit. He desired to fast and live a life of austerity, but found himself so continually offered rich and sumptuous food that he, like many of us, developed a weight problem.

In one passage which would be downright funny if it were not tragic, he recalls some particularly inept encounters with women. One was offended because he gawked too much at the ornaments on her dress; another reprimanded him when he spoke of her huge breasts "as if I liked them," and a third took offense when he almost touched one of her breasts — well, he admitted, maybe he did touch it. Rather than take these reprimands as hints of actual misbehavior, or at least a lack of good judgment, Rolle concluded that it was best to steer clear of women since they are so erratic and unpredictable. After all, in the instances I have just mentioned, he was concerned with the welfare of their souls. I think Elmer O'Brien, S. J., summed it up best in these words: "[Rolle], as many another before his time and since, desperately seems to have wished to be a mystic. And he thought he was. And he said he was. And nobody believes him."

In terms of *The Cloud's* symbolism, he was at the lower level of the active life, doing things — some religious, like dressing up like a hermit, some not so religious, like overeating and staring too much at women's breasts. Being at that level was not the problem; but thinking that he was practically in heaven was. By setting himself apart from the church and — in his own mind at least — above all his contemporaries in spiritual maturity, he only proved himself to be unattractively arrogant and spiritually immature.

If I am right that most of us are somewhere in the middle of things, striving on toward the perfection of real communion with God, but also backsliding into preoccupation with our daily worries, that's okay. We are in good company. Saint Paul for one knew that he was always striving on toward the goal. The really big problem is if we, like Richard Rolle, mistake where we are for where we wish we were; if we arrogate ourselves to a position of judgment of others in their spiritual endeavors.

Passion/Palm Sunday

A Tale Of Two Crosses

Luke 22:14—23:56 or Luke 23:1-49

There are two crosses juxtaposed in the Gospels. It is not the crosses that stand in such marked contrast as the responses to them. The first is a concept, a doctrine — the cross of Christian discipleship which Jesus mentions to the crowds in Luke 9:23-24: "Then he said to them all, 'If any want to become my followers, let them deny themselves and take up their cross daily and follow me. For those who want to save their life will lose it, and those who lose their life for my sake will save it.'" This teaching comes sandwiched between two of the more familiar scenes in the Gospels: Peter's confession that Jesus was indeed the Messiah, and Jesus' transfiguration six days later in which Peter, James, and John saw him with Moses and Elijah in a foreshadowing of his resurrection glory.

Framed by such awesome events, as it was, one would think that Jesus' teaching about taking up the cross would have special significance for the disciples and really sink in — at least for the closest three who were privileged to witness the transfiguration. But the Gospels remind us that it was not so simple.

As the small band continued its travels after the transfiguration, it was time for Jesus to reinforce the teaching about taking up the cross, and the Gospel says: "Let these words sink into your ears: 'The Son of Man is going to be betrayed into human hands.' But they did not understand this saying; its meaning was concealed from them, so that they could not perceive it. And they were afraid to ask him about this saying" (Luke 9:44-45).

The reason they were afraid to ask becomes painfully apparent when they arrive in Capernaum and Jesus asks the twelve what they had been arguing about as they walked along. Like children caught with their hands in the cookie jar, they were silent. Jesus knew the topic of their altercation: who among them was *greatest*.

As the group then traveled to Jerusalem for the fateful events of the last week of Jesus' earthly ministry, he again instructed them about the meaning of the cross and the cost of discipleship: "Then he took the twelve aside and said to them, 'See, we are going up to Jerusalem, and everything that is written about the Son of Man by the prophets will be accomplished. For he will be handed over to the Gentiles; and he will be mocked and insulted and spat upon. After they have flogged him, they will kill him, and on the third day he will rise again.' " (Luke 18:31-33). Almost inexplicably, James and John immediately approached Jesus asking for a favor: that one sit on his right hand in glory and the other on his left!

What the Gospels are telling us is that there were two agendas at work: Jesus' agenda of absolute obedience to God's will, obedience even unto death; and the disciples agenda of self-seeking and greatness, an agenda that might have made some sense had Jesus been the kind of military-political messiah so many were seeking, a victor who would ride into Judea like King David, throwing the Romans out. But their agenda made utterly no sense given the fact that Jesus was, on the contrary, the messiah who, like the Suffering Servant in Isaiah's prophecy, would vicariously bear the sins of the people. Following such a messiah would not bring glory and power! But in spite of the urgency and clarity of Jesus' words instructing them on the nature of discipleship, they did not want to hear; they were *afraid to ask because they didn't want to understand.*

What is perhaps most pointed about these stories is the fact that the disciples thought they had the luxury of ignoring or at least reinterpreting Jesus' words to suit their own purposes. They seemed to feel that there was some distance from the words, that these pointed teachings somehow didn't really apply to them. This, of course, is the problem with any abstract teachings — even important ideas like the "cross of discipleship" — they seem to be removed from us; they are concepts that we can control rather than the other way around.

There was nothing abstract or controllable about the wooden cross that had to be carried to Golgotha that Friday morning. It was crude and rough and heavy. None of the disciples, of course, were around that morning. They had managed the situation by running from it. No Peter; no James; no John. But there was that passerby. "As they led him away, they seized a man, Simon of Cyrene, who was coming from the country, and they laid the cross on him, and made him carry it behind Jesus" (Luke 23:26).

Any Roman soldier, of course, had the legal right to require a local to carry his gear one mile for him, something to which Jesus referred in the Sermon on the Mount. It would be analogous to a police officer commandeering your car like they do in those chase movies; you might or might not like the idea; you might agree or disagree with the police tactics; but you really would have no choice — you, like Simon of Cyrene, would be made to do it.

This scene is, of course, the very antithesis of the twelve being told that they needed to take up the cross of discipleship and then arguing about greatness. Here is the classic innocent bystander who suddenly finds himself with a cross on his shoulder. One of the hazards of being bright and of being in an academic environment is that we may begin to imagine that we can handle everything with our wits — that we are somehow immune to the trials and tribulations that affect others. We can reason or argue or talk our way out of anything — even the necessity of taking up the cross and following Christ. Not so for Simon — he was compelled.

We, of course, are sometimes made to do things too. We may be compelled by illness or circumstance, or just being in the wrong place at the right time. I trust that none of us have any delusions that we are better people or stronger Christians than those believers who continue to be persecuted for their faith in the Peoples Republic of China; or that it is because of our merit that we were not on that airliner that crashed in Peru a few years ago, as was a Southern Baptist missionary who died leaving a missionary husband and two children.

It would be nice to say that Simon of Cyrene volunteered to help with Christ's cross because he was part of the larger multitude that had followed Jesus — that's how he is portrayed in many movies and paintings. But that's not what the Scripture says. All it says is that he was "made" to carry it. It would also be nice to think that as a result of shouldering the cross Simon became a believer. But we don't know that either: it remains conjecture. But there is a fascinating clue. Readers often notice that of the three Gospels that mention Simon of Cyrene, only Mark identifies him as the "father of Alexander and Rufus." Why?

It is universally agreed that Mark's Gospel was written for the Christians in Rome facing the first great persecution under Nero. Well, at the end of his letter to these same Roman Christians, the apostle Paul includes this line: "Greet Rufus, chosen in the Lord; and greet his mother — a mother to me also" (Romans 16:13). So here, it seems clear to me, is an indication that this same Rufus and his mother — Simon's wife — had become significant enough members of the worshiping community in Rome to be singled out by Paul. This explains Mark's description of Simon as Rufus' father. I would like to think that as a result of their father and husband being drawn inextricably into the events of the Passion, this family, if not Simon himself, came to understand that Jesus was the Messiah, and to follow him.

So here are these two crosses, reminding us that there are some things in life that we control and manipulate, and others to which we must simply respond. Problems arise when we confuse the two and begin to think that we can control what we really cannot. Jesus' teaching about the need of the twelve to take up the cross and follow him was not a trial balloon, sent up by a politician to see how it would do in the polls. It is a simple statement of fact — something the disciples did not immediately grasp. They thought they could handle it.

God has chosen to give us free will, and does not coerce us into following his son, unlike the Roman soldiers who compelled Simon. But the story of Simon reminds us that the cross of discipleship is real, not just some nice idea; it requires real effort, real sacrifice, and the adoption of a really distinct lifestyle. The cross of discipleship is every bit as real as the rough hewn cross of Calvary. If we don't realize that, we are likely to look as foolish as James and John asking for special favors on the brink of the crucifixion.

Maundy Thursday

Setting
The Example

John 13:1-15

Many, many years ago — so long ago that we still showed 16 mm films in church — we used a series on the life of Jesus during Lent. The final of several films was on the Transfiguration. The part of the movie that was most meaningful to me was the beginning. In order to help the audience get into the disciples' frame of mind for what was about to happen, the movie recalled five key episodes from Jesus' Galilean ministry through rapid flashbacks: the Call of the Four Fishermen, the Call of Matthew, the Sermon on the Mount, the Centurion's Faith in requesting the healing of his servant, and the Raising of the Widow of Nain's dead son.

With all these incredible and exciting things going on, Jesus stopped on the mountainside and asked the disciples, "Who do men say that I am?" They responded with the answer we all know so well: "Some say John the Baptist, others Elijah or Jeremiah or one of the prophets." Then came the really crucial question: "But who do you say that I am?" It was one thing to be caught up in the sweep of events or the air of excitement, but quite another to make the personal profession of faith Jesus was now seeking.

We gather on Maundy Thursday caught up by another set of familiar circumstances: the setting of Holy Week. The Triumphal Entry into Jerusalem on Palm Sunday; the cleansing of the Temple; the confrontations with the religious authorities; the decision by Judas to betray his master; the Upper Room experience; the death on the cross. We have heard and read and sung interpretations of these events all our lives. No other period of the Christian Year (including Christmas) receives this kind of intense theological attention. But tonight the question for us is, what does this all *mean*? What does this death of Christ on the cross mean for me as a person? Not just in a dogmatic way, reciting the right answer to a catachetical question; not just in a historical way, getting all the facts straight. But in a personal sense, what does this death *mean to me*?

We have all, unfortunately, seen far too much of killings: ethnic cleansing and genocide, executions and assassinations, terrorist bombings and military actions. We find ourselves asking what these deaths mean. What significance should we attach to the death of a great public figure cut down by the bullet of a maniacal assassin or an international plot? And what of the deaths of so many nameless ones, whose passing goes as unnoticed by the world at large as did Jesus' death? In our day when it is so hard to see world events beyond the CNN crisis of the moment, what do these things mean?

A man's death may come suddenly, accidentally, and the meaning of it may be no more than this: that life is a fragile thing. A terrible natural disaster may have no more meaning than that given by the preacher of Ecclesiastes: "Time and chance happen to all...." A person may be executed and the meaning of his death may simply be that superior force carried him away against his will. But Jesus' death was not like that. In a variety of ways, we hear Jesus saying, "I see this coming, and I accept it for your sake" (see John 10:18).

On the night before the crucifixion Jesus tried to help his followers understand the meaning of what was happening. But he did not on this occasion use the method of the preacher, giving a sermonic lecture on the subject or speaking in parables. Instead he performed prophetic actions, like the prophets of old engaging in symbolic actions that in their own way gave notice of the true meaning of events and insight into what was about to happen. You recall Ahijah cutting the new cloak into twelve pieces, Jeremiah smashing the potter's vessel, or Hosea taking the unfaithful Gomer back to his house. Now Jesus performs some prophetic actions. What do these tell us about the meaning of his death?

The first thing he did was give a dinner and invite his closest friends. This may seem like a needless thing to say, but I think no matter how well we know this fact, it is hard for us really to get into the spirit of this evening, for most of our communion services bear no resemblance whatsoever to the Last Supper, and I would include in this most of the ritualized "Christian Seders" that have become popular in church.

For over a decade, Neu Chapel and the Hillel group at the University of Evansville have celebrated a demonstration Seder for non-Jewish students. One of the biggest problems is that many Christians come to the Seder with a certain mindset. They are appropriately reverent, saying all the prayers and going through the ritual with great solemnity. They need to be told, "You're much too stiff and formal. When we Jews celebrate the Passover, we say a prayer, then talk or laugh a bit, then we have a glass of wine, and after some more conversation we say another prayer. It's a big family thing." So if we wish to understand what this evening is all about, we must remember that these were friends gathered together to celebrate the Passover within a lively context of reflection and discussion.

Of course, it was not just a meal between friends; Jesus did not just act as a good host who provided food and drink. Something special was about to happen. But it was about to happen in a setting of warmth and friendship, acceptance and love. Jesus called his disciples his spiritual family. And here we have this family group gathered together the night before their Master's death. So whatever else Jesus' death means, it means that we can become part of this fellowship, this family of acceptance, and love. If this service tonight, or any service any time, is merely a ritual in which words are recited and gestures made, but which does not provide that feeling of emotional belonging, of love, of family, it has failed.

The synoptic Gospels focus on that special point in the meal when Jesus took the bread and broke it and gave it to each one then took a single cup of wine and passed it to each one in turn. What was special was that the same food and the same cup were shared. He gave it to them. As we think about the meaning of Jesus' death, we realize that this was a profound sharing, not just a sharing of food.

It is this image that makes Jesus' death so different from the brutal deaths of so many hundreds of thousands of others who have been executed throughout history. Jesus' life was not taken from him; it was given for his friends. He shared his life with others in the ultimate sense. And as we gather around this table, we get the message with the original twelve that somehow we are called to share in this act of giving our lives for others as Jesus did.

This is the focus of tonight's gospel, with the details of Jesus washing the disciples' feet right after dinner, apparently after sharing food. Jesus shared himself like a slave, the servant who comes in to wash the feet of guests reclining at table, an individual hardly noticed and whose service is scarcely acknowledged. But it is humble service that is pleasing to the Father.

Part of the meaning of Jesus' death for us is that we are called to be willing to die for one another, to share our lives in the ultimate sense. For more than a few in the twentieth century that literally meant martyrdom. For many it means sharing our lives a little at a time, dying many little deaths for others in servanthood: in giving what we would rather keep; in doing tasks we really don't like and do not find personally gratifying, but which are for the common good, in Jesus' name. Sharing in the blood of the new covenant would be a hollow ritual indeed if we did not pledge ourselves to observe the new commandment Jesus gave: "Love one another, just as I have loved you, you also must love one another" (13:34).

The third aspect of this meal that helps us find meaning in Jesus' death is that it is set in a context of very real human weakness and misunderstanding. Not surprisingly, Peter unintentionally articulates the problem. He cannot bear to have Jesus act as a mere servant — less or more would be acceptable — but not an abject servant. But Jesus answered, "Unless I wash you, you have no share with me" (13:8b). Even in this late hour of life the Lord bears with Peter and the others with incredible patience and reminds them that their relationships are not to be modeled on "business as usual" (v. 15).

The meaning of Christ's death becomes a little clearer. It is not just that "Jesus died to free us from sin." which he did. But it shows us how he freed us and what he frees us for. Christ's death was not an unfortunate incident or the unforeseen consequence of his bold public ministry. It was, on the contrary, a way in which he brings us into that fellowship of acceptance and warmth, friendship and love that characterizes the family of his disciples. It reminds us that as Christ shared himself ultimately — shared his flesh and blood — with us, we are called to share with one another. And it tells us that while we may not understand this lesson at first, it is one that is so important that Christ will not let us forget it until we put aside the ways of this world, the "normal" ways of doing things with all their concerns for status and success, and accept the ways of his kingdom, which are service and servanthood. As Christ lived and died for us, we find meaning in living and dying for others.

Good Friday

The Cross: A Symbol Of Absolutes

John 18:1—19:42

Pilate asked him, "What is truth?" (John 18:38).

The cross of Good Friday stands as a symbol of the absolute in a world where much *is* relative and where a great deal more seems *to be* relative. Pilate's question has become our question: "What is truth? What is genuine? What is absolute?" We contemporary Americans have become suspicious of givens and unconditionals and absolutes because of the way they are sometimes used dogmatically to force consensus. So many of us have completely dismissed the possibility of dealing with absolutes that we live in what is described by some as a therapeutic society. Everything, we seem to believe, can be handled in an intrapersonal, therapeutic manner.

If someone says, for example, that they are confronted by a problem, we assume the problem must be with them — they need therapy so that *they* will no longer feel like they have the problem. Someone has trouble at the office: we tell them to work on their attitude or to alter their habits or their dress; we may go so far as to advise them to quit and look for a job where they will feel more comfortable. It doesn't generally occur to us that the problem they present may have to do with an inherently immoral or evil system on the job — some absolute wrong that needs to be confronted and withstood absolutely. We tend to dismiss, in other words, the possibility of absolutes that demand response on their own terms. We tend to act as though every situation can be manipulated or managed away.

As we read the Passion story, we realize that Jesus would rather not have died on Good Friday: he was not a self-styled martyr.

That much was made clear in the Garden of Gethsemene as he prayed, "Remove this cup from me." But it was clear to him that there was an absolute necessity for his death: "Not what I want, but what you want" (Mark 14:36). He could not manipulate or wish away the necessity of facing head-on the worst that the powers of evil could muster by being absolutely faithful — faithful even unto death. "No one takes it [my life] from me, but I lay it down of my own accord. I have power to lay it down, and I have power to take it up again. I have received this command from my Father" (John 10:18). So Christ on the cross reminds us of the polarity of the eternal absolutes: absolute evil, the darkness that refuses to comprehend the light, which is absolute good, obedience to God, faithfulness even unto death.

When we neglect the presence of absolutes — as so many of us do — we are open to a great many pitfalls. Denying absolutes leads to a trivialization of both the power of evil, and the possibility of redemption. As a campus minister I frequently see students who are referred by local pastors or faculty. On a number of occasions I have counseled with individuals who have had firsthand experiences with the destructive powers of absolute evil: they have been abused by parents or trusted adults; they have been addicted to alcohol, other drugs, or illicit sex since they were very young; they have had multiple abortions or been married and divorced at incredibly early ages. They have been involved in all manner of destructive but very real change-of-the-millenium situations. Not infrequently the person who did the referring will remark: "Well, I can't believe so-and-so's story. I assume it is just an attention-getting device." Without denying that some people have active imaginations and know how to get attention, these stories are usually true. They are the results of destructive encounters with evil. Jesus was not looking for attention by going to Calvary. He was overcoming the power of death by facing it head on. And because of his victory over the forces of death and evil, we have the power, in Jesus' name, to overcome. But we cannot overcome death and destruction if we don't acknowledge their existence and point out the source of potential victory — Jesus, triumphant on the cross.

There is a second snare for us when we deny the reality of absolutes of good and evil related to this first one: it is the tendency to blame *the victims* of the powers of evil rather than offering them a way out. A number of studies over the years by social scientists have shown how tenaciously we hang onto the absurd notion that we live in a just universe. Most of us want to cling to the idea that if we just keep our noses clean and do our best we will be rewarded, that "everyone gets what they really deserve." As a consequence we end up blaming victims as if they brought the evil which befell them on themselves. How often is the rape victim still portrayed as a loose woman who was really "asking for it"? Some years ago one of my mother's friends was severely beaten by a purse snatcher. A newspaper article described her as "an elderly woman in a bad part of town," suggesting she had really brought the mugging on herself. My mother was indignant — her friend was waiting for the bus after church in her own neighborhood, something she had done for years. The fact is she was the victim of a violent crime, not its cause.

When I was campus minister at a large state university we had an ongoing support group for former members of destructive cults. One of the very difficult barriers often put in the way of persons coming out of such groups is that friends, families, even ministers and counselors, treat them as if some flaw in them was responsible for their cult involvement, rather than acknowledging that there are many pernicious groups that use manipulative techniques for their own end, literally snaring innocent victims. Instead of offering the word of grace, hope, and forgiveness which was assured by Calvary, we make the mistake of the disciples who, seeing the blind man at the temple asked, "Rabbi, who sinned?" (John 9:2). They wanted to know who was to blame, and we often blame the victim rather than the evil.

The third very common pitfall is the most insidious: it is the temptation to internalize every encounter with evil in an intrapersonal way leading to a crippling pre-occupation with self rather than a dynamic confrontation with the evil. Return a moment to our opening illustration of the person who feels uncomfortable on the job. Suppose the feelings of discomfort are due to the fact that the boss is embezzling money, or the company is fundamentally corrupt, or the product is a safety hazard and a public menace. Dealing with negative feelings too simply by means of a coping mechanism is to miss an opportunity to engage the absolutes of the world.

In the Gospels we read how Jesus repeatedly told the disciples that if they were to be faithful to him, they would have to suffer — they would have to confront the powers of evil, and that might hurt. It is hard to be on the side of good. Each time he told them this they responded in the same way. First, "they were afraid" (Mark 9:32 and 10:32) and then they engaged in inappropriate self-concern. They wondered who was greatest. They wanted special favors in the kingdom of heaven, they were jealous of others who did great things in Jesus' name. They became so concerned about themselves that the closest disciples fell asleep as Jesus agonized in the Garden; they were so caught up with their own feelings that they missed out on the cosmic confrontation between good and evil that resulted in eternal victory for those who do indeed follow Jesus in the way of faithfulness.

The cross stands as a symbol of the confrontation between absolutes — absolute good and absolute evil. It is a stark reminder of the irony of Pilate's question: there is truth; there are absolutes. It reminds us of Jesus' faithfulness even unto death and calls us beyond ourselves and our own feelings. It summons us to acknowledge and confront evil around us by claiming the good that God makes available to us in the sacrifice of his son Jesus. We affirm on this day of the church year that the victory over sin and death has been won by Christ's sacrifice on Calvary. The cross calls us to the battle that surrounds us by reminding us that God's good triumphs only as we painfully and faithfully face and overcome evil.

Easter Day

Belief Becoming

John 20:1-18

It is the universal witness of the Gospels that it was women who came and discovered the fulfilled promise of the resurrection early on that first day of the week. The stories vary, but it was always women. This is a good thing, because the women in the Gospels strike closer to where most of my friends and I are in our Christian walk than some of the more highly visible gospel figures. In the Bible story we read of a variety of circles of followers of our Lord. Most obvious, perhaps, were the twelve, chosen by Jesus. Not only did they live most intimately with him but, with a replacement for Judas, the twelve played a key role in the development of the early Church. Even within the twelve, however, there was the inner circle of Peter, James, and John who shared particular and spectacular experiences with the Master. Then came the seventy who were set out by Jesus on their work of proclaiming the Kingdom throughout the region of Galilee.

I am positive that I would not have qualified as one of the "inner circle of three" or even one of the twelve intimates. Some argue for a correspondence between the seventy and persons in full-time Christian work, but I wouldn't press that issue. I think if we are honest with ourselves most of us fit in with the "multitude" or "large crowd" of disciples, those who responded to the general challenges given by our Lord to "take up your cross and follow me."

While there were clearly no women among the twelve Apostles, and none that we know of among the seventy, there were many women in that larger crowd of disciples, some of them very close to Jesus. And while the Twelve scattered when things began to fall apart, the synoptic Gospels all attest to the fact that a group of women who had been faithful followers of Jesus kept vigil during the crucifixion. And John, in his touching scene, states that while the only male follower at the foot of the cross was the "beloved disciple," he was joined by the Virgin Mary, Mary the wife of Cleopas, and Mary Magdalene. They were some of those very faithful women who, according to the Scriptures, were not only ministered to by Jesus, but also "ministered to him" by supporting him out of their own goods. So while the women were not on the top rung of the ladder, they were there, faithfully following.

And now it is one of these three who stood by the cross, the unlikely Mary Magdalene, who finds her way to the tomb in the dark of pre-dawn. Why was she there? In the other Gospels the women came to prepare Jesus' body for burial, but no mention is made of that here. Of course, if we accept the traditional association of the Magdalene with the Mary who had anointed Jesus' feet (John 12), she had already prepared him symbolically for the tomb. But she is surprised and runs to Peter and (evidently) John with distress in her voice: "They have taken the Lord out of the tomb, and we do not know where they have laid him."

It is easy to pull these words out of context and use them as an indication of Mary's lack of faith. After all, had she not heard Jesus' predictions that on the third day he would rise? In fact, why was she at the tomb at all, we might press. She should have known that the Lord wouldn't be there! I hope you feel as I do that this line of reasoning is unfair and misses the point. Mary was not unfaithful but she was burdened down by the crushing events of the previous days. The shock of the betrayal, the apparent catastrophe of the kangaroo court, the agonizing way of the cross, and the crucifixion weighed so heavily on her mind that she could think of little else. So I can picture her confused, almost panic-stricken. This mental picture brings two things to mind. First, as much as we like to talk about God's providential care, it is always amazing, always taking us by surprise, so we have trouble accepting it. It is one thing to tell others that their suffering is a part of God's plan for them but quite another thing to believe it when we are the ones having the doubts. The Scriptures talk a good bit about a God who cares about us and provides for us even when we are unaware of God's presence. The traditional term for this is God's "prevenient grace," a subject John Wesley used to speak about frequently. When we face unexpected hard times, the shock of loss or unfortunate reversals, can we believe that the God who created the lilies of the field and who raised Jesus from death is at work even in our misery, even when we do not see God somehow creating an opportunity for good? It is hard to let go of our anxieties and allow God to break through. We are no less confused and burdened than Mary.

This image of the frenzied Magdalene also stands as a strong warning against being too hard on ourselves and others. We Christians are often far too quick to pronounce a temporary discouragement or a momentary setback "a serious loss of faith." The term "backslider" comes to our lips all too quickly. There is an aspect of childhood that none of us ever totally outgrows: a child often acts out the understandings of self that others provide. Tell a little boy he's a dunce, and he will often act like one. Treat a little girl like a holy terror, and you're likely to have one on your hands. Handle an adult like a terrible sinner, one who is unworthy of love — God's or ours — one who has fallen irrevocably from grace, and we have someone who begins to feel and act that way. This is not to say, of course, that times of discouragement or setback in faith cannot lead to more serious consequences if unattended. But it is to say that we have to be cautious about jumping in with both feet with self-righteous condemnations of others, or self-destructive introspection every time things seem a little discouraging. A few years ago a little book came out titled *Sinners in the Hands of an Angry Church* (Merrill, Dean, Zondervan, 1997). I don't want to be part of that church! Mary was puzzled. She seemed to have forgotten God's prevenient grace. But that discouragement was soon replaced by utter amazement.

Peter and John arrive in their often-portrayed foot race to the tomb. Here again the Gospel stories differ, but there are common elements: linen grave clothes rolled up neatly, but no body; angelic messengers; belief *and* disbelief, or perhaps we should say belief in the process of becoming. Notice the details. Simon enters the tomb first, but there is no comment about his state of mind. Then the writer of the Gospel enters and recalls, "He saw and believed," followed by the remarkable comment, "For as yet they did not understand the scripture, that he must rise from the dead" (20:9). He believed, but he did not fully understand.

The same is the case with Mary. When the angelic messenger asks her what is wrong, her response is identical to the message she had taken to Peter. There had been no opportunity for reflection, for absorbing what was happening. Her mind was racing in such a way that she did not recognize the resurrected Jesus. In a recent seminar, one student found Mary's lack of recognition of Jesus harder to believe than the presence of angels. One classmate suggested that the resurrected Jesus must have looked different from the earthly Lord, while another pointed out, quite perceptively, that Mary was in a garden and that she would have expected to see a gardener, and that is who she thought he was.

It seems to me that this scene puts to rest the notion that the empty tomb and the grave clothes provide some kind of "scientific proof" of the resurrection. All the empty tomb proved was that Jesus' body was gone, a fact which greatly troubled Mary. Evidence and faith are connected but not synonymous. Some persons are surprised when they study the life of C. S. Lewis and wonder how the great apologist of *Mere Christianity* could have penned the painful questioning of *A Grief Observed*. They overlook the simple fact that argument and conclusion are not the same thing; evidence and faith are not concomitant. Personal tragedy often motivates growth in belief through pain, but not always; and it does take time.

This time to absorb things is one of the primary reasons for Christian worship, and it is certainly one of the reasons for special worship on Easter. It is not the purpose of Easter celebrations to explain the Resurrection, let alone prove it scientifically, but it is our purpose to take a little time to let some of the great truth and overwhelming mystery of Easter sink in. During Lent the worship space at Patchwork Central (an urban intentional community in Evansville) is gradually filled with original works of art, many made from materials gleaned from the neighborhood. Most of the pieces are quite abstract: there are no banners with felt letters proclaiming, "He is Risen," no pictures of the rolled away stone. Instead, there are suggestive shapes that require interpretation, which take time and energy to figure out, just like real life.

We may very well come to our Easter morning worship as overwhelmed and confounded as Mary. Frankly I'd be amazed if there weren't at least some of us in that shape. And we stop, and take a moment to ponder the confusing landscape and see if we can recognize the resurrected one in our midst.

But there was one more thing. Jesus cautioned Mary, "Do not *hold on* to me." Another rendering of the Greek is, "Do not *cling* to me," with some of the negative connotations of "clinginess." She could not keep Jesus with her; they could not return to Lazarus' house; things would not go back to being as they were before. Mary didn't build a church there in the garden — that remained for later generations. But she did go out and announce to the disciples, "I have seen the Lord." Unfortunately the others had not yet seen Jesus and found this hard to accept. The twelve would not believe the story of the resurrection, Mark tells us, while Luke says that the other followers of Jesus regarded this news as an "idle tale."

Today we are not afforded the luxury of remaining in the beautifully decorated church forever, although some of us will spend the lion's share of today in church. The time comes when we must go out and proclaim this message of good news to those who do not believe, and who will ridicule the gospel of Jesus Christ — and no part of it more than the Resurrection story — as an "idle tale." But that is an inescapable part of our lives as disciples of Jesus. We must echo Mary's words, "I have seen the Lord."

At first Mary was totally confounded. But that didn't last for long. Unfortunately, many of us never get past this stage. We do all right identifying with the gospel characters when they were discouraged and burdened down — we know all about that. And we are in good shape in the garden with the angel and the resurrected Jesus, having our spirits lifted, being reassured, having our faith bolstered. Who would not be in good shape this moment, with the lilies, the music, the freshness of spring! It is the going out and telling that troubles us. But that's part of the Easter story, and part of our great commission as disciples of Jesus Christ.

We know that the disciples' disbelief and confusion didn't last forever. Soon the disciples were rejoicing, and before long the process of "turning the world upside-down" was beginning. But it would never have happened if Mary and the other women had kept quiet, if they had been paralyzed by fear. One of the greatest tasks in the history of the world was entrusted to them, not the twelve, not the inner circle of three, not even the seventy. It was entrusted to these plain women. And they were, as they had been, faithful. The same task, the task of proclaiming the Resurrection and the Lordship of Jesus Christ, is entrusted to us this morning. As we rejoice, may we help others rejoice by spreading the good news that Jesus who was dead, lives again!

Easter 2

Believing Is Seeing

John 20:19-31

I attended graduate school at St. Mary's Seminary and University in Baltimore, Maryland, where the Sulpician fathers still believed in some old time virtues: discomfort and hunger. One night when I discovered that supper was gruel with a few slices of smoked sausage mixed in, I decided it was time for some finger-licking good food.

After dining at the Colonel's in downtown Baltimore, I went over to a pharmacy to make a quick purchase. As I walked in the front door, I noticed that it was unusually quiet in the store, but didn't think much about it. I stepped up to the counter and asked where I could find what I was looking for. The clerk just stared at me and said, "You're standing in the blood!" After a day of theological thinking, this sounded like some metaphorical statement and I pondered it for a minute. Again he said, "You're standing in the blood!" This time I looked down and realized, to my horror, that I was literally standing in a pool of blood. Suddenly things began to fit together. There was a side entrance to this store where a knot of people was gathered around some police cars. It suddenly became clear that the eerie silence in the pharmacy was due to the fact that I had walked in just at the conclusion of an unsuccessful robbery attempt. The clerk, menaced with a gun, had pulled out his own weapon and shot the would-be thief. And here I was, standing in the blood.

How in the world, I asked myself, could I have wandered into the place where such dramatic and dangerous events had taken place and been unaware? But then, on the other hand, how could I have known? The gunshot must have not been very loud — at least not loud enough to be heard over the normal din of the inner-city. It doesn't take much imagination to understand how innocent bystanders are often caught in the crossfire.

How in the world, generations of Christians have asked, could Thomas — the one called the twin — have not believed that Jesus had been raised from the dead? How could he have doubted the other disciples? Some commentators have even come to the farfetched conclusion that his nickname, "the twin," meant that he was "double minded" and doubted about many things, that he was not really a good disciple. But the other side of the coin is, how could he have possibly really comprehended what went on that night? After all, we might say in his defense, he wasn't there.

And it is what Thomas missed by not being present that first Easter night that is really crucial to understanding the dynamics of this story. It is not primarily that he missed seeing the resurrected Jesus. After all, in the great sweep of history, only a handful of Christians ever had that experience. More basically, he missed receiving the Holy Spirit, the indwelling presence, that agent of God that enables us to see beyond the obvious and beneath the surface, that allows us to comprehend how God is working in our lives and what is really going on the in the world.

One of the characteristics of Jesus' ministry was his keen perception of what was really going on in persons' lives and in perplexing situations. Think for a few minutes about four individuals — two women, two men — whose stories I hope are familiar from the pages of John's Gospel. All needed something that Jesus was able to supply, but more fundamentally, all yearned for their needs to be recognized.

There was the Samaritan woman Jesus met by the well in the city of Sychar. They had the famous dialogue about living water: the woman clearly thought he meant fresh, flowing water from some source other than the well, while Jesus was speaking of spiritual refreshment. "I am the living water," he said.

But at the very heart of this story is the simple fact that this woman's life was just a mess! She had had five husbands and was now living with a man to whom she was not married. Jesus knew that she was searching for something — for intimacy, for acceptance, for affirmation — in all the wrong places. What she needed was some time devoted to her inner being and her spiritual hunger. He was the one, he told her, who embodied God's unconditional love in a way that could give her life real focus and fulfillment. And she seemed to believe it. She went and told the townspeople about this man who really focused on her. Could he be the Messiah?

There was another woman whose relationship problems had become very public: the woman who had been caught in the act of adultery and who was about to be stoned to death. In that dramatic confrontation Jesus shifted the focus away from the woman, who seemed to have clearly been guilty as charged. He turned the spotlight on the self-righteous attitude of her accusers: "Let anyone among you who is without sin be the first to throw a stone at her." "Woman where are they?" he asked after the accusers had filed away. "Has no-one condemned you?... Neither do I condemn you. Go your way, and from now on do not sin again." In contrast to his conversation with the Samaritan woman, Jesus focused attention *away* from the guilty woman to her accusers. Unlike them, Jesus was more interested in redemption and rehabilitation than in punishment and death.

The two men who come to mind each had physical problems: one could not walk, the other could not see. In Jerusalem, Jesus came upon a man who had been ill for 38 years. He was at the pool of Bethesda with a crowd of invalids waiting for the waters of the pool to be troubled. The belief was that the first one in the pool when the waters were troubled would be healed. Seeing him, Jesus asked what at first seems to be an odd question: "Do you want to be made well?" But the man's answer revealed that the question was right on target. Instead of giving a straight answer, he began to complain that over the years he had always gotten the short end of the stick. No one ever helped him into the pool, he whined, and so he was never healed. We have no way of knowing what other disappointments had embittered this man over nearly four decades of infirmity. Since it was commonly assumed in the ancient world that illness was generally punishment for sin, he may have been abandoned by his family and spurned by friends. But whatever his personal history, the fact was that his lameness could not be cured until he wanted things to be different: "Do you want to be made well?" As in the case of the Samaritan woman, nothing could change until there was a change of heart.

The man who had been born blind was quite another case. As Jesus and the twelve encountered him, the disciples asked a question based on that common assumption about illness: "Rabbi, who sinned, this man or his parents, that he was born blind?" Jesus said that they were barking up the wrong tree — sin wasn't a factor at all! But his unfortunate condition *did* provide an opportunity for showing God's loving care. As the story progressed, the restoring of the man's sight really became secondary to a convoluted series of events where the religious authorities tried to find fault with Jesus. There were accusations of the man and his parents that the blindness had been faked, enabling him to panhandle without really deserving it. There were disagreements over whether the healing should have been done on the Sabbath day. All the bewildered young man could do was state the obvious: "One thing I know, that though I was blind, now I see." Unlike the woman caught in the act of adultery, there is no hint whatsoever that this blind man had any responsibility for his condition. But as in that case the religious figures of his day — whom one might think would be interested in his welfare — had a totally different and absolutely destructive agenda.

In each case we are struck by Jesus' ability to focus on the most important issue: the inner turmoil of the Samaritan woman; the self-righteous zeal of the adulterous woman's accusers; the underlying guilt of the lame man; the misplaced zeal of the blind man's antagonists. "Of course Jesus knew what was going on," someone is thinking, "he was the Messiah." But the point of today's Gospel Lesson is that Jesus promises to those who believe in him the gift of the Holy Spirit which enables us to see, as he did, and to act, bringing forgiveness, wholeness, and healing to persons.

As the resurrected Jesus spoke with the disciples, he gave them both a promise and a challenge: He breathed on them, just as God had breathed the breath of life on the lifeless Adam, and he said to them, "Receive the Holy Spirit. If you forgive the sins of any, they are forgiven them; if you retain the sins of any, they are retained"

(John 20:22-23). You have the power, Jesus says, to discern when forgiveness is needed, and to speak the words of compassion and mercy to the blind man, the troubled soul, the one needing help. You also have the power to challenge inappropriate, self-damaging and sinful behavior: to force the woman at the well to look again at her life, to require those who would stone the adulterous woman to examine their own motivations. And not only do you have the power, you need to do it. "Very truly, I tell you," Jesus said in his farewell discourse, "the one who believes in me will also do the works that I do and, in fact, will do greater works than these" (John 14:12). If you have been empowered by God through the Holy Spirit to continue the ministry of Jesus and don't, then who will?

During the season of Lent and especially around Easter, many people think about the life and times of Jesus, thanks partly to the glut of biblical epics on television. But the truth is that many of us bracket the biblical narrative off from our everyday life. "If I had lived in Bible times ... if I had seen the miracles...." We make the Thomas mistake of imagining that seeing is believing. Today's Gospel Lesson turns that idea on its head. The Holy Spirit enables us — no it compels us — to see as Jesus saw and do as Jesus did. Believing is seeing: the gift of the Holy Spirit allows us *really* to comprehend what is going on around us and understand the positive role God wants us to play.

The December 6, 1992, *Manchester Guardian* carried the story of Black, a two-year-old sheep dog. The dog was left by its master, a French artisan, with a cousin in northeast France while he went to work as a traveling construction worker. After working jobs in a number of locations, he ended up in Avignon, some 500 miles from where he left Black. As you are probably guessing, he heard reports about a stray dog behaving oddly. Sure enough when the worker arrived at the pound, he was almost bowled over by Black, who had finally caught up with his master. Ralph Whitlock, the *Guardian* writer, gave this explanation for Black's ability to follow his master over a long, unpredictable, and erratic route: "The dog's sense of direction was not centred on any geographical location, but was locked on his master."

When we "lock" on Jesus Christ — when we are spiritually and mentally present as Jesus breathes the Holy Spirit on us — our sense of direction will get us where we need to be. Believing is seeing.

Easter 3

Back Where It All Began

John 21:1-19

Here we are, after the resurrection, after a couple of dramatic appearances to some of the disciples, and now we find ourselves back where it all began. We are back at the Sea of Galilee — John calls it by its other name, the Sea of Tiberias — where Jesus had called his first disciples and told them that they would be fishing for people. Nathaniel is here, just as he was when Jesus first called disciples in John 1. The truth is we haven't heard a whole lot about Nathaniel in between; and there is Peter, but Jesus calls him "Simon, son of John," a name we haven't heard since that first encounter between him and Jesus at the beginning of the story. And of course, they are up to their old trade, fishing, and like fishermen from time immemorial, they are having no luck.

Then this voice cries out, "Cast the net on the other side — throw it to the right!" Now this in itself was not remarkable; often someone standing on the fairly steep hills overlooking the Sea of Tiberias had a better view of things in the water than fishermen in the boats. Without the glare of the sun reflecting in their faces, from that elevated vantage point someone could often spot a school of fish — in fact fishermen occasionally sent someone to stand up on the hillside and direct them. What is remarkable, of course, is what a dramatic haul they make when they follow Jesus' directions, and only then do the beloved disciple and Peter realize that it is the resurrected Lord.

The symbolism here is straightforward — and John's Gospel is always highly symbolic. Without Jesus' guidance, they catch nothing; with Jesus' they have a remarkable catch — 153 fish. "I am the vine, you are the branches," Jesus had said earlier, "apart from me, you can do nothing." Today's story reinforced that truth. Even after the pain of the cross, we are not left out on a limb — the resurrected Lord Jesus is with us!

Why is that number recorded? Obviously it may be recorded because there were exactly 153 fish. But it is worth noting that according to Greek biologists of that time, there were 153 varieties of fish in the known world. So, with Jesus' guidance, they have symbolically caught a perfect number of fish — every conceivable kind of fish; a reminder that when we are faithful to Jesus Christ, when we follow Jesus' direction, we can have an enormous impact on all different kinds of people in every conceivable circumstance. In a society which has now gone through over a decade of subtle but real economic, racial, and social polarization, this image of *every conceivable kind of person* drawn together by the Lordship of Jesus Christ is very powerful.

But another key point in this story — so obvious that we may overlook it — is that the fishermen had to do something. They had to follow Jesus' advice: they actually had to lug the net up out of the sea and throw it out on the other side of the boat. A number of influential Protestant clergy — including Robert Schuller of the Crystal Cathedral in Garden Grove California — have worried in recent years about a trend for much contemporary Protestant worship and preaching to get stuck at the "pre-evangelization phase" of Christian discipleship — "Wouldn't it be grand *really* to follow Jesus! Wouldn't it be wonderful to grow in your discipleship!" "What a joy it would be if we had a more Christian nation!" Such inspirational theorizing is great; but there comes a point where you actually need to *do something* about it.

The reason that the Reverend Schuller is particularly concerned about getting stuck at this "pre-evangelization phase" is that it is a particular danger for the electronic church or very large superchurches where no one really knows anyone else. Especially in that setting, Christianity can very easily become a spectator sport with marvelous music and inspirational speaking, but not much definite expectation. Nobody really knows anybody else well enough to be specific enough to say, "Pull up your net and throw it out on the right side!"

This is the reason that through the chapel and religious groups like Kappa Chi we stress local service projects as well as national and international mission trips. They are opportunities actually to try something specific — maybe something that you have never done before, but that you feel that the Lord may be calling you to do. I'm very pleased that this summer several UE students will be involved in full-time mission work: in inner city St. Louis, in downtown Philadelphia, at the Heifer Project Livestock and Learning Center in Arkansas, and with the United Methodist Short-term missionary program. I'm pleased both because the work is valuable in itself, and also because it will give these students the opportunity to explore possibilities for later in their lives. One of my own experiences in mission and outreach work is discovering abilities and strengths of which I was unaware until they were really called for. Beginning in the fall, we will be even more systematic in offering a variety of opportunities for all of us to throw our nets on the other side, and try something different in service to Christ and serving other people in little simple ways: working in a soup kitchen, helping at the House of Bread and Peace, working at Patchwork Central. We offer these opportunities because Jesus Christ does not just call us to get teary-eyed and emotional, but to *do something.* "Throw your net on the other side!"

As this story goes on we are struck that while the setting is the same, and while the characters are the same, some things really have changed. There is a charcoal fire on the beach. The last charcoal fire we heard about in the Gospel narrative was the one in the high priest's courtyard, the one where Peter warmed himself as he denied knowing Jesus for the third and final time. Now, as they share a community breakfast which has obvious similarities to the community meal we will share in a few minutes — Jesus is after all the host of both — Peter has an opportunity to assert his love for Jesus three times. The fact that Peter, who had failed Jesus in a *really* big way, was given this opportunity for yet another chance is a great encouragement to any of us who fail Jesus. But there is a little catch.

"Simon, son of John," Jesus says, "do you love me more than *these*?" I guess the standard interpretation of this question is, "Do you love me more than these other fellows love me?" But the word "these" is just as ambiguous in the Greek text as in the English. This question could just as well mean — and I am inclined to think it does mean — "Do you love me more than you love *these things:* these people, these surroundings, these fishing boats? Are you really willing to make the significant changes in your life — to take the risks, to follow the commands — that will be necessary *really* to show your love for me? Do you love me more than *these*?"

So, here we are today, in a familiar-looking place with some familiar-looking people. And Jesus Christ is asking us, "Do you love me more than these?" Are you really willing to follow Jesus Christ in your life? Are you willing to throw the net on the other side when there may very well be family and friends on shore shouting, "Leave the net where it is! Leave well enough alone!" Are you willing to risk and change and grow? "Do you love me?"

Jesus ends with the same words with which he began: "Follow me."

Easter 4

The Father And I Are One

John 10:22-30

The year my son was in the eighth grade he came home with all kinds of stories about the class bully's exploits: he beat up classmates; he destroyed things; he even had physical confrontations with teachers. He would be punished; he would be suspended; but the behavior kept up. Hearing all these tales, I had naturally conjured up an image of this guy in my mind. When the evening for fall open house arrived, my son, my wife, and I were seated in homeroom when in came this short, square-shaped stocky student with a crew cut. Tim nudged us; there he was, the class bully — not looking anything like I had expected. And he was accompanied by a short, square-shaped stocky man with a crew cut.

As the hour for the evening program arrived, the homeroom teacher came in and immediately the adult half of this twosome went up and began belligerently asking why his son had been in some particular trouble. Almost before the teacher could respond, the father had given her a good shove — an Elaine Benis two-handed shove to the chest — but not in the same friendly manner of the Seinfeld character. It sent the teacher back against the blackboard. I recall there was shouting and some other parents and teachers getting involved and before long father and son were ushered out of the school. If I had had any questions about the relationship between these two, the behavior of the one so matched that of the other that there was no doubt in my mind which one was the chip off the other block(head).

I hope that no one is agitated that this experience came to my mind after reading today's Gospel Lesson, because I don't want anyone drawing wrong parallels or wrong conclusions other than this: while the physical appearance of these two was a tip-off to their relationship, the real clincher was their behavior: in this case unfortunately regrettable behavior. All the details are different, but it seems to me that this is the fundamental meaning of the line which is the dénouement of today's reading: "The father and I are one." What did Jesus mean by that? How do we understand him?

"The father and I are one." In the big picture, this phrase came to lie at the very heart of all kinds of controversies over the metaphysical relationship of Jesus the Nazarene to God the Father; controversies that came to be spelled out in detailed doctrines and which, to a large extent, were responsible for divisions, both East and West and within the Eastern churches. And my guess is that if we were to conduct a poll in the congregation of any American church, large or small, we would find considerable diversity of opinion about the relationship of Jesus to God the Father and the whole question of the Trinity. Those big picture questions are legitimate and important, but I don't think have much to do with this line from John's Gospel: "The father and I are one."

According to John, Jesus had been in Jerusalem for some time, saying things and doing things, and it was in response to this activity that questions had arisen. Think of a couple of the incidents which had immediately preceded today's reading in John. There is the story of the woman caught in the act of adultery who was to be stoned by her accusers. (This story is, of course, not in most of the ancient manuscripts, but it is in the *textus receptus* of John.) Jesus calls not for adherence to the letter of the law which would have called for her death, but for compassion, not unlike that found in the life and legacy of Hosea the prophet. "You judge by human standards," he said in the remarks following that confrontation. "I judge no one. Yet even if I do judge, my judgment is valid; for it is not I alone who judge, but I and the Father who sent me" (John 8:15-16). He was asserting that his verdict of compassion and his offering of a second chance was the judgment of God. "You know neither me nor my Father. If you knew me, you would know my Father also." Clearly, he is speaking about recognizing the loving, redeeming power of God in his life and words, in his *gracious* judgment.

Then there was the remarkable incident with the man born blind (in John 9) which is told in such delightful detail. It is one of my favorite stories in John. You will recall how Jesus healed the man, but, as happened with other healings, this action of bringing wholeness where there had been brokeness was soon overshadowed by concern with religious practice; the healing had occurred on the Sabbath day. So there was a series of confrontations between the authorities, the man who had been born blind, and his parents. The authorities tried to bully the parents into saying that the fellow had never really been blind at all, but a faker, duping people into giving him money for all those years. In a scenario that would be laughable if it weren't tragic, he is pushed into making the profoundly simple observation, "One thing I do know, that though I was blind, now I see."

A woman is saved from an unjust punishment and given a second chance at life; a man has his sight restored and now may begin anew; in each case it is Jesus who brings peace, healing, and new life; in each case it is the religious establishment who opposes him and seeks to maintain the *status quo* of a legal correctness and ritual purity that overlook the human tragedy involved. It is that brand of piety that loses sight of the forest of human suffering and need as it surveys the trees of institutional religion.

So by the time Jesus begins to speak of himself as the Good Shepherd in John 10 it should be clear to us what is going on, even if it was legitimately difficult for his original audience. He is the *good* shepherd who is willing to take care of his flock regardless of the cost to himself. This, of course, is in contrast to the religious leaders who Jesus characterizes as "hired hands," understandably more concerned about their own welfare than of the sheep they were supposed to be tending, but who belonged to someone else.

Had the religious leaders wanted to stone that woman just out of meanness or misogyny? Were they so jaundiced that they could not believe the man had really been blind all those years, but that the only possible explanation was that the cover for his scam had been blown? Perhaps, but I would prefer to think that most of these leaders had simply gotten off the right path somehow. Some, like the Sadducees, were quite concerned with playing ball with the

Roman authorities who granted them power and privileges. Many Pharisees had become so concerned with upholding the law as they interpreted it that the underlying principles of justice, righteousness, mercy, and redemption had somehow been obscured if not forgotten. Their concern for others had simply been overridden by self-concern. It happens.

Now it is winter and Jesus is in Jerusalem for Chanukah. And a crowd gathers around with a bad question they think sounds good: "How long will you keep us in suspense? If you are the Messiah, tell us plainly" (John 10:24). It reminds me of another bad question that sounded good, one that came from quite a different source and with very different motivation. The question brought to Jesus by the disciples of John the Baptist in Matthew's Gospel: "Are you the one who is to come, or are we to wait for another?" (Matthew 11:13). Remember Jesus' answer then? "Go and tell John what you hear and see: the blind receive their sight, the lame walk, the lepers are cleansed, the deaf hear, the dead are raised, and the poor have good news brought to them. And blessed is anyone who takes no offense at me." Now Jesus says the same thing in more theological terms: "I have told you, and you do not believe. The works that I do in my Father's name testify to me ... The Father and I are one." What could be more simple? What could be more complex?

The dissonance between expectation and reality, between what the religious leaders looked for in a messianic figure and what they saw in Jesus did not have anything to do with Jesus taking a wrong fork in the road: it had everything to do with their misunderstanding and misinterpretation of what a messiah would be like and *what God was like.* By envisioning a God captive to a set of laws, a God more concerned with vengeance than redemption, with punishment than salvation, Jesus' actions appeared incongruous. For those who caught a glimmer of "grace upon grace" it was not so mysterious. It was their misunderstanding of the nature of God that made Jesus incomprehensible, not the other way around.

The idea that some persons, particularly those with a vested interest in maintaining the institutional *status quo*, should have a distorted view of God in which vengeance and power are more important than grace and mercy is not surprising. It has always been that way: prophets were stoned before Jesus and ever since. It is why Christian institutions have so often had to reinvent the Jesus of the Gospels. Sometimes he is transformed into precisely the kind of king or CEO with secular power that Jesus explicitly rejected when he said, "My kingdom is not of this world" (John 18:36). This allows the church and Christian people to grasp after the very kind of power that Jesus explicitly warns against. Sometimes Jesus is imaged as nothing more than a substitutionary sacrifice whose only purpose was to die. This allows us to adhere to a legalistic, vengeful conception of God that ignores the life, ministry, and teachings of Jesus, that completely overlooks the fact that "the father and I are one."

Recognizing this at the beginning of our new millennium is of extreme importance, it seems to me, because it is these distorted images of Jesus, based on and encouraging a distorted view of God, which bombard us. It often seems that the everyday faith and practice of the large majority of graceful and spirit-filled Christians who engage in small acts of kindness, forgiveness, and healing is marginalized and often invisible due to the media's acceptance of the extreme Religious Right as the "real Christians." The legalistic Pharisees and power hungry Sadducees are still with us. This phenomenon, well portrayed in Bruce Bawer's 1997 book *Stealing Jesus* (Crown Publishing) is a major problem for the under thirty population which has little loyalty to and understanding of the historic mainstream of Christianity. The portrayal of the church as predominated by bigoted and mean-spirited, single-issue individuals is an enormous impediment to the spread of scriptural Christianity and a holistic gospel. This idea of "church" suggests that the universe is controlled by a vindictive God who plays favorites, rather than the God of Jesus who delights in the forgiveness of sin and the healing of maladies.

It was sad but true that the bully in my son's classroom, like many troubled people, revealed a great deal about his father. It is our joy and delight that Jesus reveals a great deal about his. What he reveals is a God of love, wholeness, holiness, and forgiveness. Many religious leaders of Jesus' day had trouble recognizing this God; many still do. But the wonderful resurrection news of this Easter season is that "the Father and I are one."

Easter 5

Rebecca's Creed

John 13:31-35

A couple of summers ago my wife and I took a twenty-fifth anniversary trip to visit friends in New Mexico and Colorado and to see places we had never seen before. One of the very enjoyable "tourist-type" things we did was to ride the famous Durango to Silverton Narrow Gauge Railroad. Originally built to haul heavy mining equipment and ore during the gold rush days, the old steam locomotives have been used in any number of western films. Today it is a scenic three-hour ride from Durango to Silverton where you spend a few hours having lunch and shopping or looking in windows (depending on whether you are male or female) and then reboard for the scenic ride back. It was a very nice day.

Unfortunately, within a couple of days the local paper had the story of a mishap of a six-year-old boy playing near the tracks of the train in Durango. He was struck as the slow-moving engine passed and was seen staggering off. Concerned, the railroad notified police and the local emergency room. Sure enough, a youngster showed up with injuries which he said were from a fall, but which the emergency room doctor said were much more compatible with a confrontation with heavy equipment. The part of the article that really caught my attention was when it continued to tell how the boy's parents were summoned to the hospital where, according to the paper, in an inebriated state, they denied that the boy was their son. "Our son is a good boy," they were quoted as saying, "he would not do something bad like this."

You hear stories about people abandoning their children, but this really struck home, maybe because we were on vacation and it really had time to sink in. It's no wonder that people are so cynical about the world. This sort of thing, of course, is the reason that many individuals feel that male imagery for God — particularly referring to God as father — is not always helpful. What about those people who have been abused, abandoned, and hurt by their fathers; what does this say to them about God?

But there is another side to this that often hits us square in the face on our international mission trips when we visit places in the world where people have more than ample reason to be cynical and embittered. In May, 1997, 22 of us from The University of Evansville spent three weeks in Africa, mostly in South Africa. Even though the apartheid system has now been officially abandoned, its legacy is clearly seen everywhere. In Cape Town you can visit District Six, an area of the city in which, for several generations, black, colored, and white, Christians and Muslims, lived together in harmony. But in the 1960s, when the machinery of apartheid moved into high gear, the area was bulldozed with the intention of creating a "White's Only" enclave. So determined was the government to eradicate any memory of peoples from different ethnic groups living together in harmony that the very streets were torn up and a new grid of streets laid down with new names. The very memory of the place was to be blotted out! The whites never moved in, and District Six still stands as a blight in the heart of beautiful Cape Town.

The truth is even without apartheid things are still bad. For the most part, colored and black citizens of South Africa do not have the economic wherewithal to move out of the townships and formerly segregated areas. It is not being cynical to point out that one of biggest changes in the last few years is that persons who were formerly destitute and homeless in the townships can now be destitute and homeless in formerly white-only areas.

And yet we found amongst the people not just an enormous pride in their beautiful homeland and the unexpectedly relatively non-violent transition it has made from white-only rule to multiracial government, but an amazingly buoyant sense of hope. *Hope!* Why is this? Is it simply national pride? Is it the charismatic and inspiring figure of Nelson Mandela? No doubt those are factors.

But something else struck me on our very first night on the streets of Cape Town. We were introduced to a gnarled old street woman who had staked out her sleeping spot on the steps of the Central Methodist Mission. She embraced one of our students who shared her name — Rebecca; she became emotional when she discovered another student shared the name of "her dead son." She introduced herself with these words: "My name is Rebecca. I believe in God. And that's why I believe in people."

"I believe in God. And that's why I believe in people." On the one hand, this disenfranchised woman, whose people had been subject to indignities and inhumanities we can barely comprehend, had every reason to be embittered and cynical. And yet she can say that she believes in people! The reason, of course, is the starting point: "I believe in God. And that's why I believe in people." Can it really be that simple? Or that profound?

It is no coincidence that all of the great historical creeds of the church begin, "I Believe in God." Only after considering the person and work of Christ and the ongoing presence of the Holy Spirit do they get around to the church and the communion of saints. It is no coincidence, because if we start out by looking at people and institutions — even the church — we are in big trouble. Only if we start with God are things put in their proper perspective.

This takes us back to the Fatherhood of God issue. If we define God in terms of human fatherhood, we may well end up with an image of God who is vindictive or arbitrary, abandoning, faithless, or worse. The point is that we do *not* define God; when we describe God as Father, we should be defining human parenthood. Genesis says that humans are created in the image of God, not the other way around.

Jesus calls us to have "eyes that seeing perceive and ears that hear and understand," and promises us that through the transforming power of the Holy Spirit we will come to see the world from God's point of view; all too often, we see God from the world's point of view.

In his book *A Simple, Decent Place to Live,* Millard Fuller talks about his early business career in the 1960s.

> *From the very beginning of our business partnership, my partner and I shared one overriding purpose:* To make a pile of money. *We were not particular about how we did it; we just wanted to be independently rich. During the eight years we were partners, we never wavered from that resolve ... So when the company treasurer marched into my office one day in 1964 to announce that I was worth a million dollars, I wasn't surprised.*
> *"What's your next goal?" she asked.*
> *"Why, ten million," I answered, "Why not?"*

His was the ultimate American success story. But Fuller goes on to describe the price that this singular focus began to exact, first on his personal integrity, then on his health, and finally on his marriage. Only when his wife, Linda, left him, informing him that the Lincoln, a large house plus a cottage on the lake, two speed boats and a maid didn't make up for his absence from her life and that of his children, did he realize what he had sacrificed for money.

Fuller goes on to describe the transformation that occurred in his life through his association with Clarence Jordan, founder of Koinonia Farms, a multi-racial Christian community in Georgia. "Millard," Jordan said to Fuller one day, "I don't have anything up my sleeve, but perhaps God has something up his sleeve for both of us." As long as he just "looked around" for role models and lifestyles, all that he could focus on was accumulating more stuff. But as Fuller began to focus more on God and God's desire for all humankind and less on human patterns of success and wealth, he developed what is surely one of the major transforming forces around the world today, Habitat for Humanity. "I believe in God — and that's why I believe in people."

Now, all of this may seem to go without saying, but I am saying it because of the great danger in always beginning by looking around, by seeing how others are doing, by looking for love in all the wrong places, even as people of God. Not long ago I read some tips for successful churches, and one of things that jumped out at me was that, according to this expert anyway, one characteristic of a successful church is that it will "place more emphasis on increasing the number of members instead of trying to increase the commitment of existing members." Without a doubt, this is the way of marketing; but is it the way of Christ? To whom do we look for models?

Dag Hammarskjold was born in 1905, the son of the Prime Minister of Sweden. He studied law and economics, and taught economics at the University of Stockholm. He became president of the board of the Bank of Sweden, then Minister of State, then head of the Swedish delegation to the United Nations, and finally Secretary General of the United Nations.

In 1960 the Belgian Congo (now the Republic of Congo) became independent, and civil war promptly broke out. Hammarskjold went in to negotiate a cease-fire, and was killed in a plane crash in Zambia on September 18, 1961. It was only after his death that it was discovered that for years he had kept a private journal, writing down his thoughts on the Lordship of Christ and its meaning for his life. Eventually the journal was published under the title *Markings*. In one place he wrote:

> *God does not die on the day when we cease to believe in a personal deity, but we die on the day when our lives cease to be illumined by the steady radiance, renewed daily, of a wonder, the source of which is beyond all reason.*

I can think of two other ways to make the same point:

> *I give you a new commandment, that you love one another. Just as I have loved you, you also should love one another. By this everyone will know that you are my disciples, if you have love for one another."*

> *"I believe in God; and that's why I believe in people."*

Easter 6

How Can They Do That?

John 14:23-29

On February 5, 1597, a group of Christian missionaries became the first martyrs in Japan. One contemporaneous account gives these last words from Paul Miki, one of them:

> *As I come to this supreme moment of my life,*
> *I am sure none of you would suppose I want to deceive you.*
> *And so I tell you plainly:*
> *there is no route to salvation*
> *except the one that Christians follow.*
>
> *My religion teaches me to pardon my enemies*
> *and all who have offended me.*
> *I do gladly pardon the emperor*
> *and all who have brought about my death,*
> *and I beg them to seek Christian baptism.*

In my ministry I have had two experiences over and over again. By way of explaining their difficulty with living a Christian life — or perhaps as a way to excuse their lack of effort — people have said something like, "Oh, if I had lived in Bible times, when Jesus was performing miracles and walking on the water, then I could have believed; but things are so different now." Most of us nod knowingly when we hear this because we can empathize with this feeling; maybe we have thought it or said it ourselves.

And I have had the privilege of working side by side with Christians in the third world — Africa, Mexico, Central and South America — who were caught in the grips of absolute poverty and awful disease, who lived in huts made of sticks and mud, and yet who possessed a profound sense of the presence of Christ, and a deep and transforming Christian joy. What is our reaction to that? Very often persons who have shared in these short-term missions will describe it as being one of the most profound experiences of their lives; and for many it has been a formative moment that has led to a life of service. Just as we knowingly nod our heads in the former case, here we sometimes shake our heads and mutter, "How can they do that?"

We dare not romanticize the poverty and suffering out of which these inspirational examples emerge, as if there is something magical about living in desperation; nor do we dare trivialize their plight (as is so easy to do) as if the main reason for the existence of these individuals is to provide inspirational footage for our mission video. And we know that this suffering does not automatically produce sainthood; for every person in these circumstances who is led to a life of servanthood, giving all they have to others, there is one who becomes self-obsessed, taking anything that is not nailed down.

This difference was made clear in one sprawling slum on the edge of a large Brazilian city. Before there was any kind of sanitary sewage system or source of safe drinking water, there were makeshift huts selling the local version of moonshine. "The quickest ticket out of the slums," as one missionary put it. In that same slum was the tiny church in which we were working; in the congregation was an elderly, blind guitar player who accompanied the singing. Well, he actually didn't *accompany* the singing because he was a terrible instrumentalist; indeed the singing proceeded more or less in spite of him. It certainly shattered any stereotypes of all Latinos being talented at this sort of thing, and I will confess that I wondered why the congregation put up with him. One night I found out. We were sharing testimonials, and here was his.

> *"As you all know, when my wife died I felt absolutely lost; it seemed that I had no reason to live. And then when I lost my eyesight, I was utterly overcome. But then Brother _____ gave me his guitar, and I discovered that I could play and help with the singing and*

praise God in this way; suddenly, I had a reason to live! And now I can glorify God in my music."

How could he do this? How could he get on with a seemingly empty and pointless life? In his own words, because he discovered God in the midst of his suffering *and* he found a way to share the presence of God in his life with others. In John 14 Jesus promises the presence of the Holy Spirit, the Advocate who will teach us all things. How does that teaching relate to all this? Maybe in a way it doesn't, although clearly the presence of the Holy Spirit does.

A few years ago, when my daughter was a student at American University in Washington, D.C., she told me about a conversation she had with a friend's aunt, a very devout Christian. This aunt's faith very much revolved around two doctrines: the Virgin Birth and the verbal inerrancy of Scripture in the original manuscripts. Upon learning that Genevieve's father was a United Methodist preacher-type, she wanted to know how many times Genevieve could recall her father preaching on either of these key doctrines. The horrifying answer was "none." The aunt suggested that perhaps her father's faith was suspect, and Genevieve's dad was one big hypocrite. In her version of things, my daughter came to my defense (although parents always do wonder what children say behind their backs!).

There is, as it happens, a good reason why I have never preached a whole sermon on either of these topics, and maybe not as many as I could have about the doctrine of the Advocate, and it is neither ignorance nor disregard. It is, rather, that in Scripture while the miraculous nature of Jesus' birth is mentioned several times, and while the *trustworthiness* of the witness of Scripture is assumed, neither of these doctrines is the focal point in the Bible that it is in many person's thinking. The focal point is much more experiential.

Indeed, when these teachings come up, it is always in the broad sweep of the "big picture" of salvation history and inevitably aimed at encouraging persons to make or strengthen their commitment to God, through Jesus Christ. This is true in the Gospel of John, in New Testament preaching, and in the theologizing of Paul.

The book of Acts contains accounts of the very earliest Christian preaching, beginning with Peter's sermon immediately following the coming of the Holy Spirit on the Day of Pentecost. I have always understood the account of that sermon in Acts, like all the sermons, to be a kind of outline or "executive summary," maybe because I can't imagine Peter and Paul speaking for only a few minutes. But in the sermon, we find certain key ideas that come up again and again:

a) Jesus was recognizable as a servant of God by his remarkable life of deeds of power, signs, and wonders.
b) It was God's will that Jesus be given over to the powers of evil and destruction; his death represented God's self-giving love and Jesus' absolute obedience, not a triumph of good over evil.
c) God vindicated Jesus by raising him from the dead, a fact attested to by firsthand witnesses.
d) *The witness and ministry of Jesus is now continued by the power and presence of the Holy Spirit;* and
e) God has, through the act of vindication, made Jesus both ruler and Messiah; in other words, the one through whom God's desire for a parent/child relationship with humankind is made available for all people everywhere.

We find all these basic points in Peter's speech at the house of Cornelius in Acts 10, with more emphasis on Jesus' post-resurrection appearances; we even find most of them in the very brief summary of the remarks Peter made in Acts 4 when he and John were first arrested and brought before the council of rulers in Jerusalem.

The longest — and first fatal — sermon in the New Testament is that delivered by the deacon and first martyr Stephen in Acts 7 where he begins at the beginning, giving a detailed recollection of the various ways in which God had reached out to humankind through a variety of servants beginning with Abraham and Moses, continuing through David and Solomon, the various prophets and finally Jesus of Nazareth. Just as they had rejected the message of all these spokespersons, and they had rejected that of Jesus when he was in the flesh, they had now stopped their ears to the witness of the Holy Spirit in their time, he argued.

What is immediately obvious about all these sermons is that none of them was given to argue the fine points — or for that matter even the gross points — of doctrine. Each was geared toward grabbing the listeners and confronting them with the choice of whether or not to accept the fact that Jesus of Nazareth was Savior and Lord and to make the appropriate life changes. It is preaching for decision. When the crowds heard Peter on Pentecost they were "cut to the heart" the text says and asked what they should do; as a result 3,000 were baptized. The council of elders were not convinced by Peter's defense, but were sufficiently impressed by its power that they feared doing him harm. Stephen, of course, did not fare so well, and was stoned to death for delivering his scathing indictment of the religious establishment. In each case, the hearers realized that they were being put on the spot.

The beautiful Christ-hymn of Philippians 2 is generally regarded as one of the most magnificent and profound statements of Christian theology, speaking of the pre-existent Christ emptying himself to become a human being and willingly dying on the cross; the hymn's content is strikingly similar to the sermons in Acts. And so is its purpose: to open believers up to the power of God at work in their lives, so that they might become vehicles of God's will in this world by "let(ting) the same mind be in you that was in Christ Jesus...."

When one has recognized Jesus as Lord and Messiah, I would assert, when one has the mind of childship, humility, obedience, and self-giving is present in a person, when one understands the welfare of others to be more important than the welfare of oneself, the fine points of doctrine will take care of themselves. But, the history of Christianity is riddled with disasters that have resulted when debates about doctrine — even crucial valid doctrines — have taken center stage resulting in divisions and excommunications and anything else but "in humility regarding others as better than yourselves."

At the University of Evansville we have a SEARCH Retreat program. SEARCH is the college level retreat with roots in the Cursillo Movement. For 48 hours, students leave campus and through a series of talks, reflections, sharing and receiving Holy

Communion, experience a sense of Christian community, some for the very first time. They experience what it means to be accepted by God and others as a worthwhile individual, with gifts to share. One student, who had been active in church and church camping all the while he grew up, sent me a note after his SEARCH experience: "In case you didn't know the SEARCH retreat was the most important thing that has happened in my life. You see the retreat opened me up to the Lord really for the first time in my life. I had such a wonderful experience that I want everyone to go."

Over the years we have received many similar testimonials. SEARCH is not magic, we hear the same thing from persons who have attended Marriage Encounter, Cursillo, Walk to Emmaus and a score of similar opportunities to open oneself to the power and presence of Jesus Christ continued through the presence of the Holy Spirit. This is the peace that Jesus promised; it is the presence of the Holy Spirit of which Peter preached; it is the same mind that was in Christ Jesus which can now be in us.

It is this mind, this presence, this power that enables us to transcend and overcome whatever situation in which we may find ourselves. It is often the answer to that question, "How can they do that?"

Ascension Of Our Lord

Living Vertically

Luke 24:44-53

Some years ago I attended a conference on the East Coast which concluded on Saturday but to save airfare I stayed over to leave on Sunday. Perusing the local paper I noted the services at the two churches within walking distance. At the United Methodist Church a local seminary professor would be preaching on "Messages from the *Journals* of John Wesley," a topic a United Methodist would almost feel compelled to hear. But at the Episcopal Church the local Bishop, John Shelby Spong, would be preaching and confirming new members. I had heard *of* Bishop Spong, but had not heard him or yet read any of his books, so I opted for ecumenism.

It was Ascension Sunday and he preached on today's text. In spite of what I had heard, he had neither tail, horns, nor pitchfork. His message was inspiring and, it seemed to me, orthodox. But I did understand what would rile some persons up. He began by pointing out how our expectations often color our perceptions: we see what we expect to see. This is why eyewitnesses to crimes and even video tapes are often less reliable than we might expect. We don't objectively see what actually happened; we see what we expect to see. Well, the Bishop reminded us, in New Testament times, and for a long time afterward, persons thought of creation as the familiar three-tiered universe, with the flat earth supported by some kind of structure over the underworld and covered by the dome-shaped firmament beyond which were the heavens. It is no surprise that in describing what happened when Jesus departed from the disciples, Luke uses "up and down" terminology, saying that "Jesus was carried up into heaven," giving rise to the traditional portrayals of Jesus rising — like a helium balloon someone has said — until he disappeared from their sight. Whether or not we would describe what happened that day using such "up and down" language is anybody's guess.

All the evangelists were, after all, using everyday language to describe extraordinary events. The Jesus who had been crucified was now alive and with the disciples in a palpable, real way. He had been raised, the tomb was empty, *and yet* John tells us that Mary could not hold on to him because he had not yet ascended to the Father. In the familiar story of "Doubting Thomas" Jesus appears in a room to which the door was shut but offers Thomas the opportunity to place his finger and hand in Jesus' wounds, suggesting that the resurrected Jesus had some attributes of his old earthly body, but not all. Luke presents the same dichotomy. On the road to Emmaus, Jesus walked alongside Cleopas and his companion unrecognized; only when he blessed and broke the bread did they realize who he was. Why were their eyes "kept from recognizing him" until that crucial moment? In the introduction to today's reading, Jesus emphasized the way in which his resurrected body was corporeal: "Look at my hands and my feet; see that it is I myself. Touch me and see; for a ghost does not have flesh and bones as you see that I have," he told the disciples before devouring a piece of broiled fish. *But* your normal everyday corporeal body does not rise from the tomb leaving grave clothes behind. It may eat a piece of fish, but it does not withdraw "up into heaven."

The danger in all of this is that we fail to note the struggle the evangelists themselves were having in describing events that fell outside the realm of normal experience and, therefore, normal language. The man Jesus, who they knew had been dead and buried, had somehow come back from the dead and made his unique identifiable presence known to them — and yet there were some differences. And now, on this fateful Ascension Day, he was with them and then he was not with them, and they knew that he had been taken to heaven. In Acts 1, when Luke reiterates this Ascension story, the connection between Jesus' leaving and the coming of the Holy Spirit is spelled out. John's Gospel made the connection even clearer: "... the Advocate, the Holy Spirit, whom the

Father will send in my name, will teach you everything, and remind you of all that I have said to you" (14:26). So here is the reality that the disciples experienced. Jesus of Nazareth had been with them as a person; he did remarkable things to be sure, but he was a person. He was killed. But then, amazingly, Jesus returned from the grave and in ways that challenged their senses and pushed the envelope of everyday language made himself known to them. Finally, Jesus was present with them in an entirely new way through the indwelling presence and guidance of the Holy Spirit.

The problem with all of this is, naturally, that most of us don't want to struggle and grapple with things. In a recent political campaign in Indiana one candidate described public education in the state as "slow and easy," and meant it as a compliment! I have to admit grudgingly that he was on to a basic human trait. We want things straight and easy; we want either/or not both/and. From the earliest days of Christianity there have been many believers who have made one choice or the other. There have been those (the *Docetics*) who have protected the divinity of Jesus by refusing to accept that he was really, fully human; he may have looked human, he may have appeared to suffer, but not really. While this position has been a heresy for generations, it is still around in plenty of popular Christian literature. On the other hand, much (but by no means all) of the contemporary interest in the historical Jesus regards him as one of history's seminal figures, but no more. To hold the two together in tension is always more difficult than opting for one or the other, which is perhaps why so many of us have done the latter. The story of the ascension, as fraught with difficulties as it may be, challenges our Christian commitment to the core because it reminds us that we must get beyond easy answers and be willing to push the boundaries of our understanding.

In a recent book (*Reason in Faith,* Paulist Press, 1999) Adriaan Peperzak suggests three dimensions of what he calls the "heart of religion," which I think address the challenge in today's lesson. Our religion, he writes, should be *comprehensive*, an experience of the whole of reality insofar as it pertains to the experiencing subject; *radical*, as an experience of ultimate meaning; and *dynamic*, not static, but an ongoing movement oriented by God (p. 64). If there is one thing today's lesson presents, it is the radicality of our faith; because we are dealing with that which is deepest, highest, and most profound in our lives, the ordinary language we use to describe everyday events breaks down. How do we describe the overwhelming experience of the movement of God's spirit in our lives? This is something mystics have been grappling with for millennia and which is particularly difficult in our day of reductionism. A "heart strangely warmed" becomes heartburn; a Damascus Road experience, an epileptic seizure; a vision or voice, a delusion and sign of mental unbalance; a "dark night of the soul," clinical depression.

We may opt for giving up the struggle and concluding that these critiques are largely correct, that the answer to Peggy Lee's old sung question, "Is that all there is?" is "Yes, pretty much." Oh, we might cling to a belief in or hope for an afterlife, and we might pray in really dire situations, but pretty much give up on trying to articulate, or even expect, truly radical experiences of God's presence. Some of us may even engage in a Christian reductionism of our own: the only proof of a true relationship with God is speaking in tongues, or intellectual assent to certain doctrines, or a particular "plan of salvation," or a set sacramental system. To expect more or other is wrong, damaging, and heretical. It is no wonder that our Christian faith has become a privatized matter indeed; not only can we not talk much about it in an unbelieving world, we hesitate to say too much in the community of faith.

Many weeks ago, at the very beginning of Lent, I mentioned a 1958 article by the great German/American theologian Paul Tillich in the then very popular *Saturday Evening Post* magazine titled, "The Lost Dimension in Religion." The lost dimension about which Tillich fretted in that article was the dimension of depth, living life for that which is other than the immediate, loudest, most pressing concern, that world that is "too much with us," of which Auden wrote. You may recall (probably not, but indulge me) that as we began the season of Lent I suggested that if the distractions of the modern world take over our lives, we are destined to live life superficially, horizontally as it were, rather than at the ultimate levels Tillich urged. Now, after making our way through the forty days of Lent and much of the Season of Easter we see that this modern distraction is compounded by the great difficulty we have in allowing the extraordinary into our ordinary world; in expressing the radical wonder that must be a part of an authentic Christian commitment. If we cannot share in the breathless marvel of those disciples who experienced the risen Jesus with them and then suddenly being taken to heaven — share not explain — how can we hope to enter into the "fullness" of life of which Jesus spoke? This is where the comprehensiveness of our faith comes in. Our faith, according to Peperzak, should be *comprehensive*, that is an experience of the whole of reality insofar as it pertains to the experiencing subject. We are marvelous and complex beings, a bundle of thoughts, intuitions, emotions, fears, hopes, dreads, and so on. When we Christians speak of the abundant life, we should not be limiting ourselves, as we often do, to certain aspects or dimensions of life: just the "spiritual" or only the intrapersonal or perhaps just the institutional; it means everything, a comprehensive faith. This is easy to say and hard to accept. Today's newspaper has the headline, "Faith helps crash victim," as though it is news that religious faith should help anybody with anything. As a young pastor I became very interested in the totality of our beings, particularly as I visited isolated parishioners, alone in their homes or institutions. I recall being quite excited when, in 1977, I attended a seminar where hard scientific data was presented on the strong connection between the emotional, spiritual, and physical. I soon read the then new book *The Broken Heart: The Medical Consequences of Loneliness* by Dr. James J. Lynch (Basic Books, 1977). I now know that this influential study was neither the first nor the last work to draw these strong connections. Yet a quarter century later these ideas have not had any great impact in the Christian community (while they have been more widely embraced by some new age and holistic healing movements). In 1977 I would not have thought that stories of the impact of faith, belief, prayer, or supportive community would have still been grist for human interest stories in the new millenium. Insofar as our faith is less than comprehensive, forcing us to stretch across categories, to re-examine our ways of thinking, to grope for words and concepts to articulate what we know to be true, it is less than the Ascension faith; we are living horizontally, not vertically.

As our faith becomes more comprehensive, less bound by the limitations of language and culture, it will clearly be *dynamic*, not static, but an ongoing movement oriented by God. Not long ago I was part of a group that was discussing the need for a new outreach ministry in our community, aftercare for persons released from prison, clearly the kind of ministry best sponsored by a coalition of churches rather than a single congregation. In the course of the conversation I remarked on how difficult it often seemed to be to get such cooperative ventures off the ground. By way of explanation one layman remarked that it was because so many congregations in our area are "highly organized, internal" churches whose main function is to care for the believers within the congregation. That may be an explanation, but it is hardly a justification. The ministering to and maintaining members is an important function of any local church, but when the maintenance of the *status quo* becomes the exclusive purpose, it is a problem. As individuals and groups of Christians we are always on the road to perfection, to paraphrase John Wesley. When we live vertically, constantly exploring the height and depth, the length and breadth of God's riches, we always have to be on the move, always exploring new depths of commitment and avenues of service. Theologically, biblically, an "internal" church is not a church; a static, unidimensional horizontal life is not a Christian life.

Good Friday challenged the disciples to rethink everything. How could they understand who Jesus was and all that he had done after the ignominious death on the cross? Then Easter Day and the resurrection appearance on the road, in the upper room, at the lakeside all challenged the disciples to rethink everything again. How could they understand who Jesus was and all that he had done and was doing in view of his ongoing presence with them? And now, on the day of the Ascension, as Jesus is with them, and then not with them, in a way that they know signals his entry into glory were the disciples challenged to rethink everything yet again! How could they understand who Jesus was and all that he had done and would do now that he was taken from them in this cosmic manner?

And we know that when the Day of Pentecost arrived the disciples had to rethink everything yet one more time. Rethinking, grasping and groping for words, creating new categories of thought and new images of life and faith, this is what living vertically is all about. Living vertically is radical, comprehensive, and dynamic because it cannot settle for the definitions of the culture, or reductionism or the *status quo*. It is always exploring new dimensions in God's power and grace.

As we explore the depths of God's love in our lives, we will encounter the same things those first disciples did. We will have to think and rethink, define and redefine, invent new words and new categories of thought. We will be puzzled and surprised. But like them, we will worship, be filled with great joy, and find ourselves continually blessing God.

Easter 7

Christo-centric Or Ego-centric?

John 17:20-26

Have you ever noticed that some constellations are named for animals that they don't really resemble? If you have ever been in the Scouts or taken a course in astronomy or just looked up into the sky at night, you know what I am talking about. As an undergraduate astronomy minor at Brown University, many years ago, I would give tours at the Ladd Observatory and on clear nights point out constellations from the outdoor gallery. But people often were not satisfied. For example, the stars in the constellation Ursa Major, The Great Bear, do not look the part. There's no bear there, as far as I can see. Where is the bear — hibernating? We could just as well call it the Great Figure Eight or the Large Ostrich.

People often deal with this problem one of two ways. The first is to suggest that while the ancient people who named the constellations — the ancient Greeks, Romans, and Egyptians — may have thought they saw the outlines of familiar animals in the heavens, it was because they were so superstitious or just downright stupid that they didn't know the difference between a Bear, a Figure Eight, and an Ostrich. Or it is suggested that *you* are too stupid to see the outline of the bear that is clearly sitting there in the sky, and that if you'd just pay more attention or squint a little harder or maybe write a special report, you would soon enough see the bear.

Both of these common-sensical responses are examples of intellectual dishonesty, not dealing with the data that present themselves in an open-minded and probing manner. The first solution, that the ancients were simply dumber than we are, is an example of what the great Christian writer and Oxford don C. S. Lewis referred to as Chronological Arrogance — assuming that we always possess more and better knowledge of all things than earlier, more "primitive" people. If something earlier people thought doesn't make sense to us, they are *ipso facto* wrong: they could not possibly have anything to teach us! Of course we don't just do this with earlier people, we do it with any group that we consider beyond the bounds of acceptable thought — what my 83-year-old mother would call "normal people." That might include other nations or cultures, other racial groups, other branches of Christianity, or just other socio-economic groups within our own town. If they think or say or do something that doesn't make immediate sense to me, that is not transparently obvious in my frame of references, it is because they are aberrant, stupid, wrong, or otherwise misinformed.

The second approach — that you are just not looking closely enough — is the Blame Game: if you don't see the Bear then it is because you are just not trying, or the one asking you is not asking in the proper manner, or the person who suggested you look at constellations is a sadist, and someone is to blame for this and someone will pay! If we come up with more standardized tests for people looking at constellations or more rigorous training for observatory guides — or perhaps licensing them — the problem of not seeing the bear will disappear. In the meantime I can see some lawsuit potential here.

The point is, as many of you know, that neither of these common and evidently satisfying responses is correct. To paraphrase Shakespeare, the fault, dear reader, is not in our stars. It is in our position in relation to those stars. Because of movements, both of the stars themselves and of the earth, the groupings of stars that suggested the shapes of animals, or other objects, to the ancient Greeks, Romans, and Egyptians simply don't look the same as they used to. It is as simple, or as complex, as that. There is neither blame nor fault at work, but there is a need to read a book, look up a web site, or ask a question.

How often we do this to one another in the Christian community! Let me give you three examples dealing with the doctrine of the Holy Spirit. One of our brightest and most articulate pre-ministerial students of recent years came from a Pentecostal background.

She found the spiritual gift of tongues to be a great blessing, primarily in private devotions. When she began to inquire about seminary education and ordination in her branch of Christianity, she was asked if she affirmed that the gift of speaking in tongues is the most important spiritual gift and the only true proof of salvation: that if one does not speak in tongues, one is not a real Christian. She indicated, in absolute honesty, that she could not accept that position based either on her detailed study of the New Testament or her experience of the contemporary Christian community. She was told that there would be no place for her in that particular denomination.

At the other extreme, some years ago we had a guest resource for a series of Christian lectures at the campus I was serving. He was a high-ranking pastor in a particular denomination which we shall call the Jonesites. He described an occasion when a person came forward after an altar call and began sobbing and rocking back and forth. This pastor told how he went up to this individual, placed his hands on both shoulders in order to stop his rocking and said, "We don't do that in Jonesite churches!" This, he explained, because he felt that such an outburst might precede speaking in tongues which *is always demonic in origin*. (He had thoughtfully brought along a supply of booklets he had written warning about the demonic origin of tongues.) Lest anyone think that this kind of issue would never affect a middle-of-the-road mainliner like me, I preached not long ago at the Branchville State Prison on the topic of Christian decision making and referred in my sermon to being led by the Holy Spirit. I could see from his body language that this really bothered one of the other volunteers in attendance that evening. Following the service I made a little small-talk and asked from what church he came. He was a member of a well-known area church which I would describe as being quite anti-Pentecostal. Evidently this anti-Pentecostalism had been taken to the extreme of being uncomfortable with any reference to the Holy Spirit who, the last time I checked, was still part of the Trinity and whose job description entails companionship and guidance for believers.

The question, of course, is: How does this kind of divisive attitude which assumes that any viewpoint, any practice other than my own is somehow misinformed, perverse, and just wrong, fit in with Jesus' prayer: "The glory that you have given me I have given them, so that they may be one, as we are one ..." (John 17:22)? As near as I can tell, the answer is that it does not fit in. The three examples I have cited are each, in their own way, cases of intellectual and spiritual arrogance and dishonesty. If we as Christians are to provide the kind of unified witness Jesus prayed for, we must work harder to understand and appreciate the Christian experiences of others, rather than dismiss or denigrate them.

This arrogance and dishonesty is one of the banes of the educated: we assume that because we are smart, observant, and well-informed things should simply be obvious to us, that we can fairly well size up any situation without really trying.

Some years ago my brother-in-law, his wife, and I volunteered to deliver Christmas dinners to homebound persons for the Little Brothers of the Poor on the North Side of Chicago. We went to some tough and discouraging places, none more so than a walk-up one-room apartment. A man of perhaps fifty was lying on a bed in the middle of the room. He had only one leg, and there was a pair of crutches leaning unused in the corner. We spoke a little bit about his troubles: not being able to get around, losing his job, and so on.

Finally, in my best pastoral style, I asked how he had happened to lose his leg. "What!" he asked angrily. "How did you lose your leg?" "I didn't lose any leg," he told me in no uncertain terms. "I was born with one leg. Getting around with one leg is no problem. A fellow can do just fine with one leg. Losing a leg!?" Eventually my Ph.D. psychologist brother-in-law gave me a little help by asking why he was bedfast. It turned out he was one of the very small percentage of men who suffer from breast cancer, and he had radical surgery to remove the cancer which had required the removal of lymph nodes and some muscles in his armpits and shoulders. For the first time in his life, he was unable to use crutches, the crutches that had always enabled him to get around, hold down a job, and be self-sufficient. As he made clear, a fellow with one leg can do just fine!

The arrogance on my part, of course, was assuming that I could size things up without asking any questions. I mean how smart do you have to be: a middle-aged guy with one leg who complains that he can't get around? Well, you have to be smarter than I acted that day.

It reminded me of an occasion when I was with a mission team in Brazil where we had the opportunity to worship a few times in a small Methodist church in a slum. At the first few services the unaccompanied singing was quite enthusiastic and moving, so at a weeknight service when an older, blind gentleman arrived, I thought we were in for a special treat. As the service commenced he began to strum on the guitar and *he was awful.* If there was any connection between his playing and the congregation's singing, it escaped me. What in the world was happening?

When it was time for testimonies, we went around the congregation sharing blessings from the Lord. "You all know me," the guitarist began. Every head in the congregation nodded. "When my wife died, I didn't know what I would do! Then when I lost my eyesight, I was in absolute despair. But the Lord gave me the gift of this guitar, and now I have a reason to live. I can come and play and praise the Lord." "Amen," the congregation responded, "Praise God! Hallelujah! Glory to God!" I, of course, felt about two inches tall, as I should have. What I misperceived as a musical moment, they understood to be a spiritual transformation. I could tell this guy couldn't play the guitar worth a lick; they could see the glory of God revealed in Jesus Christ, glory revealed to this man because God has loved us through Jesus Christ before the foundation of the world (John 17:24).

Nowhere is intellectual and spiritual arrogance more common or more dangerous than in issues of motivation: *why* people, institutions, and nations do what they do; *how* situations got to a certain point; *what* could have been done differently. Because we seldom have access to persons' innermost thoughts we are left to make judgments based only on rather superficial information. But even then, if we take into account the big picture — motivation, ideology — we can avoid the pitfalls of superficial judgments. In his book *The Greatest Generation* (Random House, 1998) the journalist Tom Brokaw does that with my father's generation, those who fought WW II. Let me quote from the introduction to his book.

> *At a time in their lives when their days and nights should have been filled with innocent adventure, love, and the lessons of the workaday world, they were fighting in the most primitive conditions possible across the bloodied landscape of France, Belgium, Italy, Austria, and the coral islands of the Pacific. They answered the call to save the world from the two most powerful and ruthless military machines ever assembled, instruments of conquest in the hands of fascist maniacs. They faced great odds and a late start, but they did not protest. They succeeded on every front. They won the war; they saved the world. They came home to joyous and shortlived celebrations and immediately began the task of rebuilding their lives and the world they wanted.*

Is Brokaw overly sentimental and romantic? Perhaps in some cases he is. But without some comprehension of "answering the call to save the world," so much about those years makes no sense at all.

Joshua Lawrence Chamberlain[1] was "the Hero of Little Round Top." He commanded Union troops that held out against a massive Confederate charge against that knoll at Gettysburg on July 3, 1863. Eventually he was awarded the Congressional Medal of Honor for his valor at Little Round Top. He went on to fight in many other major battles of the war between the states and was wounded three times (on one occasion the field surgeon pronounced him mortally wounded). But he lived and ended the war as a Brigadier General. Later in life he served four terms as Governor of Maine and for a time was President of Bowdoin College.

From where did this war hero come? Joshua Lawrence Chamberlain was Professor of Rhetoric at Bowdoin College in Maine at the outbreak of the Civil War. A graduate of Bowdoin and Bangor Theological Seminary he, like many Northerners and some Southerners, was very much opposed to slavery. His conviction that all persons were created by God and equal in God's sight had been nurtured during his undergraduate years at Bowdoin through contact with a professor's wife who was working on a novel and discussing its progress with groups of students — what we today would call focus groups. The book was *Uncle Tom's Cabin* and she was Harriet Beecher Stowe.

Once the war broke out, Chamberlain determined that the best way he could live out his deeply-held value of human equality was to enlist in the Union Army. While the Bowdoin faculty presumably shared his anti-slavery sentiment, they turned down his request for a leave of absence to enlist in the Union forces. They felt that his presence on campus was more important than a role he could play in the military. Undaunted, Chamberlain applied for a two-year study leave, which was readily granted. What he decided to study was how to serve in the Union Army.

It would be easy, given a brief history book entry on Chamberlain, to assume that he was an opportunist, someone who went to war to launch a political career: we have heard of many such people. But we know from his diaries and letters that as a governor and college president, he always looked back to that day on a rocky spot in Pennsylvania as *the* defining moment in his life. It was at that instant that the value he said was most important to him — fundamental, God-given human equality — was put to the ultimate test. Things did not just happen to Chamberlain; he was not swept up by powers beyond his control. He was right where he meant to be. He had deeply held Christian values, and when it became necessary, they guided his actions.

How often we ignore or even impugn the motivations of our fellow Christians. As a child I was taught that the prayers uttered at the church down the street never rose above the ceiling because the people who worshiped there were just a "country club church." As an adult I have heard that Mother Teresa was not a real Christian; and who can forget Jerry Falwell's immortal observation prior to the fall of apartheid in South Africa, that the black folks were really happy and Bishop Desmond Tutu was just "phony"?

In a world that does not know God (John 17:25), it is imperative that we constantly lift up the stories of the saints who have been compelled by the values of our faith; but we so often doubt each other's motives.

I recall the day my son Tim, then in the eighth grade, came home from school aggravated over their social studies lesson on

Dr. Martin Luther King, Jr. "You would have never guessed he was a preacher," he said. So we sat down and went through his text. He was right. From the presentation there, and evidently in class as well, there was mention of neither Jesus Christ nor the Church, nor was the influence of the teachings of Mohandas Ghandi even hinted. King, from that textbook, was evidently some kind of activist or organizer who got a lot of folks behind him. One would never guess the Church had anything to do with the Civil Rights Movement.

We often complain that the media does a poor job of portraying Christians. A student was recently interviewed on the "bias of the media against religious people." She felt, and I agree, that it is not so much a bias as a blind spot. When Christians are portrayed at all it is often as crooks, perverts, or hypocrites. There seems to be self-censorship when it comes to dealing with sincere, deeply-held religious motivation. Unfortunately it seems to me that we cannot simply blame the media if we continue to beat up on each other. In an industry that is driven by acceptance and ratings, it is little wonder they avoid matters that seem so contentious even *within the Christian family*. So we actually mitigate against Jesus' prayer that our unity of witness shine out in an unbelieving world.

Jesus' prayer in John 17 portrays a church life which is Christocentric, centered on Jesus who himself is centered in the Father. Our mutual love as Christians, found in Jesus' mutuality with the Father, is to be a beacon in a dark and unbelieving world. Too often, however, we have made a church life which is ego-centric: centered on me and those just like me. We have allowed intellectual and spiritual arrogance to separate ourselves from our sisters and brothers in Christ. Worse than that, we have often felt good about it, because we assume that our limited understanding is perfect; that looking at people superficially, we can read and judge their faith and their motivations.

---

1. For a different and more detailed treatment of Chamberlain, see my *The Backside of God and Other Occasional Sermons* (CSS Publishing Company, 2000) p. 81f.

Books In This Cycle C Series

GOSPEL SET

Praying For A Whole New World
Sermons For Advent/Christmas/Epiphany
William G. Carter

Living Vertically
Sermons For Lent/Easter
John N. Brittain

Changing A Paradigm — Or Two
Sermons For Sundays After Pentecost (First Third)
Glenn E. Ludwig

Topsy-Turvy: Living In The Biblical World
Sermons For Sundays After Pentecost (Middle Third)
Thomas A. Renquist

Ten Hits, One Run, Nine Errors
Sermons For Sundays After Pentecost (Last Third)
John E. Berger

FIRST LESSON SET

The Presence In The Promise
Sermons For Advent/Christmas/Epiphany
Harry N. Huxhold

Deformed, Disfigured, And Despised
Sermons For Lent/Easter
Carlyle Fielding Stewart III

Two Kings And Three Prophets For Less Than A Quarter
Sermons For Sundays After Pentecost (First Third)
Robert Leslie Holmes

What If What They Say Is True?
Sermons For Sundays After Pentecost (Middle Third)
John W. Wurster

A Word That Sets Free
Sermons For Sundays After Pentecost (Last Third)
Mark Ellingsen

SECOND LESSON SET
You Have Mail From God!
Sermons For Advent/Christmas/Epiphany
Harold C. Warlick, Jr.

Hope For The Weary Heart
Sermons For Lent/Easter
Henry F. Woodruff

A Hope That Does Not Disappoint
Sermons For Sundays After Pentecost (First Third)
Billy D. Strayhorn

Big Lessons From Little-Known Letters
Sermons For Sundays After Pentecost (Middle Third)
Kirk W. Webster

Don't Forget This!
Robert R. Kopp
Sermons For Sundays After Pentecost (Last Third)

www.ingramcontent.com/pod-product-compliance
Lightning Source LLC
Chambersburg PA
CBHW071718040426
42446CB00011B/2117